Lawyers and Reporters

Understanding and Working with the Media

Robert L. Rothman, Editor

Section of Litigation

Defending Liberty
Pursuing Justice

Lawyers and the media / [edited by] Robert L. Rothman.
    p. cm.
Includes index.
ISBN 1-57073-763-0
1. Lawyers—Public relations—United States. I. Rothman, Robert L., 1953–

KF298.L39 1999
959.2'934—dc21   99-53098
                                                        CIP

Summary of Contents

Contents

CHAPTER 4
Ground Rules for Communication
Gail Appleson **43**

CHAPTER 5
"Off-the-Record" versus "On-the-Record" Comments
Alan Abrahamson **51**

DELIVERING THE MESSAGE

CHAPTER 6
The Art of Public Relations for Lawyers
Jill Lewis **59**

CHAPTER 7
Writing Press Releases
Jill Lewis   **75**

CHAPTER 8
Media Interviews: How to Appear Confident and in Control
Spring Asher and Marilyn Ringo   **83**

THE LAWYERS

CHAPTER 9
Litigation That Attracts the Media
Peter C. Canfield   95

CHAPTER 10
Think Before You Leap: Talking to the Media
Paul Mark Sandler   101

CHAPTER 14
Unpopular Clients or Causes and the Media
Jeffrey O. Bramlett and Paul H. Schwartz   **137**

CHAPTER 15
Judges and the Media
Hilton Fuller   **149**

CONCLUSION

CHAPTER 16
A Small Step for Lawyers and Journalists, a
Giant Step for the Law: Winning Back Public Respect
Lewis Wolfson   **159**

About the Editor

Robert L Rothman is a partner in the Atlanta law firm of Arnall Golden & Gregory, L.L.P. He is chair of the firm's Litigation Department, where his practice includes general commercial litigation and media law. He received his J.D. with highest honors in 1982 from the Florida State University College of Law, where he was Editor-in-Chief of the *Law Review,* and his B.S. with high honors in 1974 from the University of Florida College of Journalism and Communications. Mr. Rothman was chair of the first Georgia Bar, Media, and Judiciary Conference, and continues to serve on the conference planning committee. He has served as a member of the ABA Section of Litigation Council and presently is co-director of the Section of Litigation's Publications Division. Before attending law school, he was a newspaper reporter for several Florida newspapers, including a three-and-one-half-year stint in the state capitol bureau of *The Tampa Tribune.*

About the Contributors

Alan Abrahamson has been a staff writer for the *Los Angeles Times* since 1989. He is a 1980 graduate of the Medill School of Journalism at Northwestern University in Evanston, Illinois. He received his J.D. from the University of California's Hastings College of Law in San Francisco in 1987, and is a member of the state bar of California. He and his wife, Laura, are the proud parents of three children: Kayla, Bobby, and Rachel.

Gail Appleson has been a professional journalist since 1973. Her experience includes writing for daily, weekly, and monthly publications including the *ABA Journal* and the *National Law Journal.* She joined Reuters in 1985 and was named its first national law correspondent in 1990. While at Reuters, she has been the lead reporter covering a number of high-profile cases and legal issues including the Wall Street insider trading scandals and the government's case against Michael Milken, tobacco and gun litigation, and the World Trade Center bombing trials.

Spring Asher is a principal in Chambers & Asher Speechworks, a firm specializing in speech and media training. She is a former executive producer of *Noonday* on WXIA TV, winner of six Emmy Awards, and The Best of Gannett Award for News Programming. Her column, "Getting Ahead," coauthored with Wicke Chambers, appeared for four years in the *Atlanta Journal/Constitution* business section. Asher and Chambers have also written *Wooing & Winning*

Business (John Wiley & Sons). Speechworks clients have appeared on the *Today Show* and *60 Minutes* and in *The Wall Street Journal* and include INVESCO, Scientific-Atlanta, MCI WorldCom, Kurt Salmon Associates, Georgia-Pacific, and UPS.

Jeffrey O. Bramlett is a partner in the trial and appellate firm of Bondurant, Mixson & Elmore in Atlanta. Before joining the firm in 1981, he served as law clerk to the Hon. Jerre S. Williams on the U.S. Court of Appeals (Fifth Circuit) and as a legislative aide to U.S. Congressman Bob Eckhardt of Texas. He is a graduate of the University of Texas School of Law, where he edited the *Texas Law Review.* Bramlett is the president-elect of the Atlanta Bar Association and a member of the Board of Governors of the State Bar of Georgia. He served as president of the ACLU in Georgia, on the ACLU national Board of Directors, and as an ACLU cooperating lawyer in a variety of civil liberties controversies.

Peter C. Canfield is a partner in the Atlanta office of Dow, Lohnes & Albertson, specializing in media law and litigation. He served as a lawyer with the U.S. Department of Justice and clerked for U.S. Court of Appeals Judge Frank M. Johnson, Jr. (Eleventh Circuit) and U.S. District Judge Myron Thompson (M.D. Ala.) He received his J.D. from Yale Law School, where he was an editor of the *Yale Law Journal,* and his undergraduate degree from Amherst College, with honors, where he was an editor of the student newspaper. A founding director of the Georgia First Amendment Foundation, he is a co-chair of the libel and privacy conference presented biannually by the National Association of Broadcasters, the Newspaper Association of America, and the Libel Defense Resource Center.

Anthony E. DiResta joined the D.C. office of Fulbright & Jaworski in January of 1999. His practice focuses on complex commercial litigation, and he specializes in antitrust and unfair competition law, deceptive trade practices, and First Amendment and media litigation. Before joining the firm, he was the Director of the Southeast Regional Office of the Federal Trade Commission and practiced complex civil litigation at the trial and appellate levels. Mr. DiResta is an active member of the American Law Institute and the ABA. He received his B.A. from Rollins College, his Ed.M. from Harvard

University, and his J.D. from the College of Law of Florida State University, during which time he was an intern with the Chief Justice of the Florida Supreme Court.

Wilfredo Fernandez is an Assistant U.S. Attorney for the Southern District of Florida. He received his B.A. in Journalism and Political Science from New York University's College of Arts and Sciences. Prior to attending law school, he worked as a newspaper reporter for *The Dispatch* in New Jersey and was a freelance reporter for *The Miami Herald.* He received his J.D. from Cornell Law School, then joined the New York office of Winthrop, Stimson, Putnam & Roberts and specialized in corporate banking and commercial business transactions. Mr. Fernandez joined the U.S. Department of Justice in 1991 as an assistant in the Special Prosecutions Division where he obtained the district's first conviction of an anti-Castro terrorist group under the Arms/Export Control Act. In 1994, he was appointed Special Counsel to the U.S. Attorney and served as media spokesman under three administrations. He is currently assigned to the Economic Crimes Unit and teaches a course on legal research and writing at the University of Miami School of Law.

Hilton Fuller is a judge with the DeKalb Superior Court in Decatur, Georgia. He is a graduate of the University of Florida and Emory University. From 1964 to 1980, he conducted an active trial practice in the metropolitan Atlanta area. In 1980, he was elected as judge of the DeKalb County Superior Court, and from 1991 to 1995 he served as Chief Judge of the DeKalb County Superior Court, Stone Mountain Judicial Circuit, and Administrative Judge of the Fourth Judicial District. Judge Fuller is also a graduate of the National Judicial College (NJC) and has served on the faculties of the National Institute of Trial Advocacy, the Institute for Court Management, and the NJC. He has served as adjunct professor of law at Georgia State University and has taught trial judges from over 35 states how to manage trials more effectively. Judge Fuller is a nationally recognized authority on the relationship between the judiciary and bioethics. He served as judicial associate editor for *Courts, Health, Science and the Law,* a journal published by Georgetown University Medical and Law Center.

Jill Lewis is president of Jill Lewis Public Relations Inc., a full-service integrated marketing communications firm based in Chicago. The firm specializes in strategic public relations and marketing communications programs that assist clients nationally with practice development, issues management, and tactical visibility campaigns. Prior to founding her consulting firm, Lewis served the ABA as a public relations specialist in the Division for Media Relations and Pubic Affairs.

Lee Stapleton Milford is an Assistant U.S. Attorney for the Southern District of Florida. A prosecutor in the office since 1984, she has served as the Chief Assistant U.S. Attorney of one of the largest U.S. Attorney's Offices in the country. Recently she spent two years at the Department of Justice as the national director of the Organized Crime Drug Enforcement Task Force program. Currently a Senior Litigation Counsel in the Economic Crimes Unit, she investigates and prosecutes health care fraud cases. Ms. Milford teaches litigation skills at the University of Miami School of Law and is co-chair of the Criminal Litigation Committee of the ABA Section of Litigation. She received her undergraduate, graduate, and law degrees from the University of Florida. Prior to law school, she was a newspaper reporter and taught journalism at the University of Florida College of Journalism.

John E. Morris has been a reporter and editor with *The American Lawyer* magazine since 1993. He is based in London, where he also writes for *The Daily Deal* newspaper. Before becoming a journalist in 1990, Morris practiced law for more than six years with McCutcheon, Doyle, Brown & Enersen and the San Francisco City Attorney's Office. He graduated from Harvard Law School in 1983.

Marilyn Ringo is Vice President of Media Strategies with Chambers & Asher Speechworks, a firm specializing in speech and media training in Atlanta. She also produces and cohosts Georgia Public Television's business show, *Success Track*. She is a former news anchor for CNN *Headline News* and an Emmy Award-winning television producer and reporter. She has hosted and produced Turner Broadcasting programs including *Good News* and "Women of the '90s Report." Ms. Ringo's work has featured President Jimmy Carter, ACOG's Billy Payne, Evander Holyfield, Anne Rivers

Siddons, Martina Navratilova, as well as business executives. She holds a master's degree in Journalism and Communications.

Paul Mark Sandler is a partner in the Baltimore law firm of Freishtat & Sandler. He is an active trial lawyer representing notable clients in a variety of cases in state and federal courts. He is the coauthor of *Pattern Examinations of Witnesses for the Maryland Lawyer;* coeditor of *Appellate Practice for the Maryland Lawyer: State and Federal;* coauthor of *Pleading Causes of Action in Maryland;* and coauthor of *Model Witness Examinations* (ABA 1997). He is a frequent lecturer on trial and appellate practice.

Paul H. Schwartz is an associate in the litigation department of Cooley Godward L.L.P., and is resident in the Denver and Boulder offices. His practice is focused on all aspects of commercial litigation, including antitrust, contract, employment, intellectual property, securities, and white collar criminal defense. From 1994 to 1995, Mr. Schwartz served as law clerk to Justice Stephen Breyer and Retired Justice Harry A. Blackmun of the U.S. Supreme Court. He earlier served as law clerk to Judge Phyllis A. Kravitch, U. S. Court of Appeals for the Eleventh Circuit. Mr. Schwartz received his J.D. with Highest Honors in 1992 from the University of North Carolina School of Law, where he earned a Chancellors Scholarship and was elected to the Order of the Coif. While attending law school, Mr. Schwartz served as Editor-in-Chief of the *North Carolina Law Review.* Mr. Schwartz received his Sc.B. degree in Mechanical Engineering from Brown University.

Gregg D. Thomas has been a partner with Holland & Knight since 1982. He currently directs their media law department, which represents newspapers and television stations throughout Florida and the Southeastern United States. He successfully argued a 1990 U.S. Supreme Court case involving the First Amendment rights of a reporter (*Smith v. Butterworth*). He was part of Holland & Knight's media team that successfully sought injunctive relief against the 1988 banning of the film *The Last Temptation of Christ* in Florida. Mr. Thomas is a member of the ABA Section of Litigation and Forum on Communications Law. He is a founding chair of the Hillsborough County Bar Association's Media Law Section. He received his J.D., with honors, from the University of Florida, where he served as

Executive Editor of the Law Review. He received his B.A., magna cum laude, Phi Beta Kappa, from Vanderbilt University.

Alexander Wohl is a lawyer and writer in Washington, D.C. He is presently a speechwriter and legal counsel for U.S. Secretary of Education, Richard W. Riley, as well as an adjunct professor at the American University—both the Washington College of Law and the Department of Justice, Law and Society. Previously, he was a Judicial Fellow at the U.S. Supreme Court; a law clerk for Judge Ralph B. Guy of the U.S. Court of Appeals (Sixth Circuit); and a lawyer with the D.C. firm of Dickstein, Shapiro, Morin & Oshinsky. He has covered the Supreme Court for the *San Francisco Chronicle* and the *ABA Journal.* He is also a contributing editor for *Biography* magazine and writes regularly on the Supreme Court and legal affairs for a number of publications.

Lewis Wolfson is Professor Emeritus of Communication at American University and director of the Dialogue with the Press Program, which brings together professionals and journalists to learn more about each others' working worlds. He is a former Washington correspondent who founded American University's graduate degree programs in Journalism and Public Affairs and News Media Studies. He has taught and written extensively about Washington and national politics, public policy and the press, and conducted or participated in numerous seminars and panels. Mr. Wolfson's book, *Untapped Power of the Press,* focuses on the role the press plays in public understanding of the government. He has twice been a research fellow at Harvard University's Kennedy School of Government and published a study there of the press-government revolving door.

Ronald G. Woods has practiced federal criminal defense for 12 years in Houston, Texas. He was recently named Best Attorney in Houston by the *Houston Press* (Annual Best of Houston Issue 1999). He served four years as a Special Agent and Legal Advisor in the Federal Bureau of Investigation and 20 years as a state and federal prosecutor in Houston, including three years as U.S. Attorney for the Southern District of Texas. Mr. Woods is a graduate of the University of Texas School of Law.

Introduction

Robert L. Rothman

BY THE TIME YOUR SECRETARY tells you, "A reporter from the *Tribune* is on line one," it will be too late to read this book. Or if you pick up your own telephone and hear, "Ms. Johnson, this is Steve Smith from Channel 2 calling," you will not have time to put him on hold long enough to learn what you need to know before you take his call.

Some lawyers interact with the media regularly. These lawyers have gained a working knowledge of how reporters operate, what they want in interviews, how to best present clients' positions, and what drives the decision about whether a lawsuit is newsworthy. Those lawyers can put this book down.

On the other hand, some lawyers do not have a clue about how journalists function, and could not possibly care less. The problem with this attitude is that understanding how the media operates *before* a crisis arises may well be in your client's best interest. Lawyers tempted to say they never handle cases of interest to the media may be in for unpleasant surprises if they do not understand what makes the media tick and what creates interest in a particular lawsuit. Sometimes the lawsuit you consider *least* likely to attract media attention suddenly results in a flood of telephone calls. Sometimes the people involved in a case invite the attention, and other times the subject matter does the trick. Every now and then, it is just a slow news day and a reporter simply wants to latch on to a story.

Although you cannot always anticipate what will generate media attention, you can reasonably assume that sometime during the course of your career you will be called upon to speak for your client in front of a person wielding a camera, microphone, or notepad and pen. Your words will be recorded and used—sometimes just for background and other times for a quote—in your local newspaper or on your local televison news program. Simply waiting for that event to occur, without taking the time to learn how to use these situations to your client's best advantage, is asking for trouble. To be effective, you must learn how media personnel view their roles and approach their tasks, and understand the factors you should consider before deciding whether to take that phone call or agree to that interview.

Alexander Wohl, a lawyer, writer, and former judicial clerk, provides a basic understanding of the competing professional goals that influence the professional relationships between journalists, lawyers, and judges. Journalists and lawyers experienced in dealing with each other have contributed chapters illuminating how they approach their relationships, all for the purpose of helping you understand what is involved and at stake when—willingly or unwillingly—you find yourself representing a client in a case that will appear on the front page of tomorrow's newspaper or on the evening news. In another chapter, an experienced trial judge gives his perspective on media relationships and the impact of media in the courtroom. Public relations professionals offer tips on the best techniques for media communications, including how to initiate communications when a lawyer and client deem it appropriate. Lewis Wolfson, Professor Emeritus of Communication at American University, lends his insights on the critical need for lawyers to make a substantially greater effort at working with the media, rather than viewing them as "the enemy."

The chapters in this book speak from different perspectives and with different voices. The authors try to help you understand the reasons why lawyers and the media must and will interact, and how to use those opportunities most effectively—always for the best interest of your clients. Although the book touches on the ethical issues relating to media interaction, each lawyer must become familiar with the applicable rules in his or her jurisdiction to avoid running afoul of professional obligations.

Lawyers and Reporters: Understanding and Working with the Media is a starting point for lawyers who have not had much exposure to dealing with the media. Ultimately, as several of the writers note, the interest you serve is that of the client—not your own. And, for many clients, the reality is that winning in the court of public opinion is many times more important than winning in the judicial courtroom. This book will help prepare you for success in the "other courtroom."

Lawyers, Journalists, and Judges: Coexisting Amid Conflicting Professional Goals

Alexander Wohl

THERE WAS A TIME WHEN a volume purporting to address lawyers' dealings with the media might be placed in the "humor" section of bookstores, grouped alongside other titles belonging to the category of all-time thinnest books. Generally, the two professions have not had what can be called a close or productive relationship, with feelings about each other ranging from contempt to jealousy.[1] Efforts to change this dynamic have been largely unsuccessful.

It is a peculiar condition for two professions that each have a long and distinguished place in our nation's history, including the distinction—limited to few other occupations—of being specifically addressed in the Bill of Rights. The animosity is even more curious today, in light of the boundless opportunities and increasing prominence that both journalists and lawyers experience in our fast-paced, technologically advanced world. Rapidly growing links between law and virtually every other aspect of our communities, and an ever-expanding role for journalists at a time of instant global communications, have made these two professions increasingly indispensable to the world and each other.

Ironically, the only thing more apparent than the animosity of each profession toward the other is the hostility of the public toward both. National surveys measuring public opinion on issues such as esteem for individual professions reveal that neither lawyers nor journalists are particularly well thought of. A brief review of the many lawyer jokes reveals a similar, albeit less scientific, conclusion. In light of this shared antipathy, one might conclude (or at least hope) that lawyers and journalists would develop a means of cooperating, communicating, or even commiserating to increase understanding between the two and take advantage of the obvious mutual benefits that would result from a more productive relationship. Yet little in the way of organized cooperation exists, and the barriers and suspicions linger.

When journalists and lawyers are forced to deal professionally with one another, too often they do so reluctantly, with feelings of wariness and trepidation. And these feelings are only aggravated by of the role of judges, who are frequently the regulators, editors, and disciplinarians concerning many of the issues involved in the lawyer-journalist relationship.

Lawyers—who may be forceful and outspoken advocates for clients when it comes to drafting briefs or appearing before judges or juries—sometimes become flustered, reticent, or even tongue-tied when confronted with a microphone or a reporter with pen and notepad. Similarly, journalists—who are fearless when questioning a president or senator about some policy or indiscretion—often become confused and misguided when focusing on the intricacies of the law or the legal profession. Throw in the actions of judges—who qualify loosely as the "bosses" of these lawyers in the trenches—and you have a combustible mixture and a significant challenge for all the participants in this interchange.

A number of factors have contributed to this history of suspicion, fear, and loathing, including the differing natures, institutional cultures, and goals of the two professions, as well as the contrasting characters, personalities, and styles of the individuals who make up their memberships. Although no prototypical personality or background exists for either a journalist or a lawyer, workers in each profession often share a number of traits or tendencies because of the responsibilities, demands, and characteristics of their businesses.

The other chapters in this book explore in greater detail some of the reasons for this conflict, and offer some serious and substantive suggestions garnered through firsthand experience with these antagonisms and the resulting predicaments. This introductory chapter presents a brief overview of legal-media relations involving three integral figures—lawyers, journalists, and judges.

The Lawyer

In an occurrence as regular as the swallows returning to Capistrano, legal periodicals publish articles professing to explain how lawyers can learn to deal with the media, and how journalists and lawyers can "be friends" and "air their beefs." On the one hand, these articles offer a welcome recognition of the existence of a long-term problem and the potential benefits that warrant efforts to overcome the conflict. On the other hand, they constitute an acknowledgment that even with all this available advice, lawyers still struggle with the underlying difficulties of this interprofessional relationship.

Differing Goals and Conceptual Approaches

Many of the problems that lawyers have with journalists result from a basic lack of understanding about journalism itself. But the source of the problem goes much deeper, stemming also from the contrasting conceptual approaches that lawyers and journalists bring to their professions and the issues they must address to be successful in that profession.[2] At the heart of this contrast is the training lawyers receive, which leads them to approach their work in a fundamentally and substantively different manner than journalists. Law students are taught to shape the existing law and its interpretations into a plausible and convincing argument. (Or, as one humorous description of the law school experience suggests, it teaches just one thing—how to take two situations that are exactly the same and show how they are different. Arguably, it also teaches the reverse.) As a result, many lawyers are suspicious of what they view as the more general, superficial, or short-term nature of media reporting. Because of their orientation to detail and exhaustive research (sometimes to the point of compulsiveness), lawyers may ridicule the relatively limited background work done by a journalist for a typical story. The philosophy of billable hours, so deeply ingrained in a lawyer's psyche, offers further evidence of these differences, as it rewards laborious, lengthy, and detail-oriented work and scorns or avoids the quick and easy solution or settlement.

However, this criticism of the significant differences in legal and journalistic research fails to account for the dissimilar goals and philosophies of lawyers and journalists—providing legal representation versus gathering and reporting the news. Journalists are intent on exposing, educating, and informing (and sometimes crusading). Most like nothing better than to see big, bold headlines attached to their stories. Lawyers—albeit with some notable exceptions—desire to downplay, to conceal, and to be advocates. They want nothing less than to keep their clients' names out of the headlines.

And yet, even with these great dissimilarities, areas of common ground exist. To seize this ground and the advantages a successful relationship affords, however, requires skill, shrewdness, and hard work, as well as an awareness and understanding of journalists and their profession that few lawyers have.

Understanding and Working with Journalists to Meet Lawyers' Goals

As an associate in a law firm, I was surprised regularly by the incredulous and dismayed reactions of partners when the weekly legal newspaper would include a flawed story about the firm or one of its big clients, or, in the alternative, when it would not include any such story. I would ask the partners what they had done to promote or prevent the story. How much had they talked to the reporter? Had they returned phone calls? Had they seemed accessible? Too often they had acted as partners typically do—extremely busy, dismissive, and self-important. They would send the reporter a batch of briefs to review, or talk to the reporter in extremely technical terms, and then only after many weeks of ignoring interview requests. There seemed to be no understanding that, just as with an opposing lawyer during a difficult negotiation, a relationship needed to be developed.

Even those partners who understood the importance of establishing a productive relationship with the media were often unable to shake their lawyerly self-importance. I once arranged a meeting between a journalist friend of mine and a partner who was working on a case of some national significance. In a lengthy conference call, the partner was forthcoming and helpful, speaking in lucid prose about the case. And yet, he could not restrain himself from inserting his importance to the case and the story. When the writer published his article, all the facts were there, but the partner was hardly mentioned, clearly reflecting the journalist's reaction to such a heavy-handed effort to have extraneous material foisted on him.

Of course, even the most understated lawyer who regularly returns phone calls will not be guaranteed a job as a CNN commentator, or even a quote in a reporter's story. But in general, this kind of assistance can reap rewards. And there are many different ways in which a lawyer—even a busy lawyer—can choose to work with a journalist.

Probably the best known (and certainly the most commonly criticized) method of such communication is called "trying cases in the media"—lawyers divulging information to the media about an issue or a criminal suspect to shape public discussion and, the lawyer hopes, the legal action concerning an ongoing case. In its most common form, a prosecutor holds a press conference to discuss a crime or prosecution and outline some of the evidence and theories. The result may be a series of news articles, broadcasts, and commentary that reach a legal or moral conclusion and shape public opinion on an issue long before a trial is held, a verdict reached, or sometimes even an arrest made.[3] The tendentious publicity created by this tactic implicitly, and often explicitly, violates the integrity of our justice system—specifically the guarantees implicit in trial by jury. Equally problematic are the professional and ethical concerns lawyers face when commenting upon, and perhaps unduly influencing, pending cases.

This being said, there may be nothing wrong with more decorous efforts to inform and educate reporters about a case and even to promote, in an acceptable manner, the facts of that case from a client's viewpoint. On one level, this kind of activity is simply a question of common sense. If a case or an issue is going to receive media attention, that case will likely find that attention without a lawyer's assistance. Providing a helping hand by supplying informative, nonprejudicial background information to a journalist may benefit a client, or at least not harm the client.

On another level, media relations becomes a question of strategy. An informational briefing by a lawyer about a client's case or legal strategy that is not the focus of press attention—a sort of proactive strike against possible negative media treatment—may not only have personal and professional benefits for the lawyer and client, it arguably may also fulfill a certain civic and public educational goal by helping to inform a society that is sadly lacking in an understanding of the judiciary. To this end, certain efforts to raise the profile or issues of a case may even help fulfill the lawyer's ethical duty to "represent a client zealously within the bounds of the law."[4] All such efforts, of course, must include the knowledge and consent of the client.

On still another level, a lawyer's media work may have among its purposes advocacy of an issue not directly related to an ongoing case. For instance, media interaction can enable a lawyer to bring to a broader audience the issues the lawyer tackles in court (police misconduct against minorities, for example). As a result, media work can contribute to the administration of justice and furtherance of equal protection under the laws.[5]

Finally, a lawyer's efforts to promote a case or assist a journalist by providing information ultimately may advance that lawyer's own reputation and business. Without discussing either the constitutional implications of lawyer advertising or matters of taste, there is nothing necessarily wrong with such activity. Many lawyers fail to understand that there is no general prohibition on speaking with the media. (There are a number of exceptions and variations, of course, based on ethical rules in each jurisdiction, local court rules, and the individual responsibilities of certain lawyers, such as prosecutors.)

Moreover, in today's image-conscious world, the diligent lawyer may actually be doing a disservice to a client by failing to counter critical media portraits of that client with equivalent positive information. Being a successful lawyer today may require not only the legal skill to protect a client's interests in the courtroom, but also the savvy to win—and present the perception of winning—legal battles through the media. As one writer noted, at a time when the legal profession receives almost as much news coverage as the locker room of the New York Yankees in a pennant race,[6] a lawyer must stay competitive, and do so intelligently.

The Journalist

Virtually everyone—from lawyers to newspaper readers to editors who put articles, broadcasts, and other forms of publication into final form—has a personal, and often stereotyped, view of reporters. These views range from the cynical (as reflected in the comment credited to Mark Twain: "So I became a newspaperman. I hated to do it, but I couldn't find honest employment."), to the more noble (as enunciated in Horace Greeley's description: "Then hail to the Press! Chosen guardian of freedom! Strong sword-arm of justice! Bright sunbeam of truth!"[7]). One well-known legal publisher and journalistic critic has commented, "When it comes to arrogance and lack of accountability, journalists are probably the only people on the planet who make lawyers look good."[8]

A number of factors cause this vast range of characterizations, perhaps the most important of which is the often distorted understanding of the journalism profession. This section examines that role through discussions of the differing characteristics of workers within the profession, the goal of the profession to educate and inform, the difficulties and challenges implicit in that role, and some of the factors that guide a reporter in developing a story.

The Differing Characteristics of Journalists
The varied perceptions and understandings of journalists that are drawn and shaped from the content and context of individual

media-related interactions can affect everything from an individual's view of a specific topic, to a journalist's credibility, to a comprehensive view of the profession. In reaching these conclusions, most people fail to understand that journalism is not an exact science,[9] nor are reporters fungible. High-quality journalism requires both talent and hard work. And reporters, like most professionals, have varying ability and work ethos. They take distinct approaches to their craft and have differing interests, focuses, and attitudes.

Moreover, depending on their specific jobs, journalists have varied responsibilities. Some journalists function as news reporters, others specialize in investigative journalism, and still others write opinion and commentary. And some journalists do not even cover the same beat from day to day. A journalist employed by a general-interest publication, such as a daily city newspaper or television news show, has a role that differs from a reporter who works for one of the growing number of specialty publications, which today include cable television, desktop newsletters, and even cyber-journals transmitted solely over the Internet. Each of these "niche" publications has a targeted readership or viewership that may include individual professionals or specific segments of a profession, such as a legal newsletter about computer law.

The Profession's Goal to Educate and Inform

Notwithstanding this diversity within the profession, journalists share an underlying goal—educating the public by providing information.[10] No doubt, this charge means different things to different people. To some it is a social responsibility; to others, simply an unnecessary by-product of their work. At a minimum, however, it must be acknowledged that the job of journalists involves a transfer of knowledge about specific subjects or events. Or, as Oscar Wilde caustically put it, "Modern journalism, by giving us the opinions of the uneducated, keeps us in touch with the ignorance of the community."[11]

The role of journalist as educator, and in many cases as primary educator, is growing as our society becomes ever more dependent on the information and interpretation provided by journalists. As a result of decreasing leisure time, individuals have less opportunity to study and understand specific subjects unrelated to their daily responsibilities. Too many citizens already lack essential foundations of knowledge, particularly about our government. Increased professional specialization has accentuated the lack of understanding about areas other than one's field of work or expertise. All these factors have led to an increased reliance on the quick and easy explanations offered by the media which, too often, provide the bulk of information the public receives about a subject.

This dependence is even more striking in legal affairs, due to the technical nature of these subjects and the disproportionate impact law has on our society. Instead of encouraging a higher degree of cooperation between the professions, however, the forced interaction between lawyers and journalists resulting from increased reporting on law-related activities has accentuated the differences between the two professions.

These differences are qualitative as well as quantitative. At their core, they may be summarized by the observation that law is an occupation oriented to detail, while journalism is more focused on general interpretations. This characterization is not intended as a negative commentary on the ability of journalists. Rather, it is meant only to express that journalists, as a result of the demands of their profession, generally take a broad and active view of the events they cover, while lawyers take a more passive—even scholarly—approach to those issues. It may seem ironic to describe a lawyer's work as passive, in light of the obvious ongoing and active nature of legal representation. However, this active/passive distinction concerns, for instance, the response to a verdict, a job dismissal, or a personal injury. Lawyers may take months and sometimes years before filing an initial legal action, while journalists usually desire the details instantly and publish the story immediately.

Difficulties and Challenges Implicit in the Journalist's Role

Valid reasons exist for both the journalist's and lawyer's approaches. There is nonetheless a danger—real and perceived—that journalists, in covering the law more quickly, will not capture the big picture or the whole story. This potential problem is not reserved to coverage of legal affairs, as journalist Tom Wicker noted in discussing journalists' coverage of the Civil Rights movement during the 1960s and a concurrent story largely ignored:

> From the early fifties onward, the press amply covered the civil-rights movement with its forceful spokespeople, its marches and demonstrating, its victories and defeats, its numerous organizations; but at the same time one of the great migrations of history—of blacks from the fields of the South into the great cities of America—was changing the nature of those cities forever, while going virtually unremarked in the press until the change had been wrought. Effective as it was, the civil-rights movement—so thoroughly covered—may have had less significance than the migration—so nearly uncovered.[12]

One of the greatest challenges to understanding the journalism profession is realizing that journalism is, first and foremost, a business. Journalists do not aspire to be—in contrast to the lionized reputation advanced by some (including journalists themselves)—the "schoolmasters of the common people."[13] Though the profession may ultimately have the goal or result of educating or informing the public, for the most part the media do not exist solely for the public welfare. As the distinguished press critic, A.J. Liebling explained, "The function of the press in society is to inform, but its business role is to make money."[14] In contrast, the public perception of law is almost solely as a business, and pro bono activities are probably neither well known nor understood by the lay public.

The fact that journalism is a business means that journalists face certain limits—on story space and time, and on the ability to research and report, use detail and description, and develop themes and concepts. They must avoid the mundane, at times even to the end of sacrificing important technical details. A good news story (one that is interesting to watch, read, or hear) requires action, in the form of verdicts, scandals, or explanations; everything else is just filler. Without action, the door is open to a changed channel or a paper making its way ever more quickly to the bottom of the bird cage. Even those reporters who work for specialty publications cannot include every detail about a case or a legal issue. Instead, they must provide strong summaries, include only the most pertinent facts, and offer generalized explanations of how a decision will affect their readers, viewers, or listeners.

Like many reporters, I have felt the disappointment when a quotation, paragraph, or turn of phrase I felt was important to a story was eliminated by an editor because of space limitations. Similarly, I would be dismayed when I was told to simplify a story or to explain a court's rationale for a decision based on its effect on a certain group of readers, even when that effect was negligible or that aspect of the decision relatively insignificant. For these types of reasons, a natural antagonism often arises between reporters and editors. At the same time, a good editor has the ability to make a story and the reporter's work that much better.

Factors Considered in Developing a Story

The lack of understanding about what or how much is important to a news story is a major source of confusion and potential conflict between lawyer and journalist. Some of the factors that guide a reporter in putting together a story have little or no value to lawyers. For example, one of the most crucial elements is newsworthiness—if an event is stale or undramatic, then for the journalist's purposes it is neither interesting nor news (although which of these factors comes first is sometimes questionable). Unfortunately, many lawyers do not understand this principle, perhaps because they become so involved with their own cases that they believe their matters are the most important—not only on the court's docket, but in the public's mind. The news cycle itself is significantly different for journalists and lawyers. Consider, for example, the overwhelming coverage during allegations against President Clinton and investigations by Independent Counsel Kenneth Starr. The press required daily—and sometimes even hourly—updates on witnesses appearing before one of Starr's grand juries, which involve a drawn out process without the dramatic appeal or results of regular trials.

Closely related to "newsworthiness" is the principle of exclusivity. Notwithstanding the concept known as "pack journalism"[15] (involving swarms of reporters descending on the same story), every journalist wants a special angle or access to a story, such as a court's decision leaked ahead of time or, less dramatically, an "exclusive" interview with one of the parties in a case. Lawyers may overlook this concept, because in some ways, it runs counter to their professional training. Generally, the journalist's mission is to discover (to reveal original or previously unearthed activities), whereas the lawyer's role is to recycle (to take previous cases or situations and apply those to the matters before them).

Still another factor journalists must consider is timeliness—how quickly a story must be prepared. Most people fail to appreciate the limited time journalists often have to put together a story. Although a diligent journalist may conduct a significant amount of background research on an issue before an event occurs, frequently the event itself provides the first notice of something newsworthy. As a result, the learning curve can be steep, and anything that makes the task easier—from rapidly returned telephone calls before a deadline, to concise interview responses, to explanations without legalese—benefits the journalist, and ultimately the lawyer who wants to play a role in the story.

The term "timeliness" means various things to different types of journalists or publications. For instance, a decision by a local judge that enjoins a construction company from building is breaking news to a daily morning newspaper reporter and an important story that needs to be researched—with interviews conducted and the ramifications of the decision deciphered—by a deadline that night. The reporter may write a story of three to four typewritten pages, which might address local, state, national, political, economic, and environmental impacts. By comparison, a local television news reporter may have the same subject, but with an earlier deadline, and the opportunity to present the story in two to three minutes on the evening news. The television reporter will need to know, in addition to a cogent Gilbert's-like explanation of the issues, the effect this ruling has on the people involved and the community at large, preferably in a few one- or two-sentence sound bites. The report will require something visual, such as an on-camera interview, footage of the construction site, or pictures of the parties coming out of the courthouse. Any assistance a lawyer can provide to these ends—with an understanding of the deadlines and realities the reporter faces—is typically appreciated, and may even offer rewards to the lawyer.

The approaches of these types of journalists differ still from that of a writer for a specialty newsletter, who may have several days to dig up needed information and background. Moreover, because the lawyers who subscribe to specialty publications tend to be familiar with the area of law involved, the writer can present greater detail and explanation. A lawyer discussing a matter with a reporter from this kind of journal can expect a more sophisticated discussion, and a more sophisticated article. For this type of publication, thoroughness and foresight are usually more important than immediacy.

In each case, though, deadlines come and go with the inevitable passage of time, which often leads to feelings of frustration and exhaustion that can come from dealing with lawyers. Unreturned phone calls, time-consuming discussions about a lawyer's importance and involvement with a case, or discourse filled with legalese—all ignore the time constraints that control much of the work done by journalists. Given lawyers' preoccupation with time and deadlines, it is particularly ironic that the issue of time is a recurring problem between the two professions. But this apparent parallel seems to have done little to increase understanding or improve the relationship between lawyers and journalists.

The Judge

The final piece in this peculiar puzzle is the judge—the unique person who has the power, implicitly or explicitly, to control communication between the other two. Although journalists and lawyers have a number of opportunities to interact informally before the onset of litigation, their interaction ultimately focuses on the motions, filings, and other assorted legal skirmishes that lead up to and include a trial. This activity, including the drama and circus-like atmosphere that may surround a trial, provides the grist on which journalism thrives, and the excitement for which trial lawyers live. For the judge, the ringmaster of this "big top," there are significant pressures and potential pitfalls.

One can hardly discuss the role of judges and their interaction with lawyers and journalists today without mentioning the modern paradigm for this real-life drama, the O.J. Simpson criminal trial. Broadcast live on CNN and Court TV, and, in its early stages, on several networks, the Simpson case was billed as the "trial of the century." The broadcast, the verdict, and the impact of both on society were (and continue to be) exhaustively examined, discussed, dissected, and analyzed.[16]

Although the Simpson trial generated extraordinary scrutiny of virtually every facet of trial and pretrial procedure, as well as of media coverage of courts, this atmosphere is not unprecedented. For instance, the 1934 trial of Bruno Hauptmann, the man accused of kidnapping and murdering Charles Lindbergh's baby, was, for its time, at least equal in spectacle and attention. One commentator noted that more media representatives covered the Hauptmann trial than were sent to France to cover World War I.[17] Movie newsreels about the trial pervaded theaters everywhere, but the real revolutionary medium of that day was radio, and 40 million Americans had their new electronic boxes tuned to coverage of the trial.[18] In fact, coverage of this trial prompted the American Bar Association to adopt the since-abandoned Canon 35 of the Code of Judicial Conduct, prohibiting judges from permitting the broadcast or still photographs of courtroom proceedings.[19] In both these landmark trials, few participants were left unscathed or untarnished. And in both cases, sitting at the center of controversy and commentary was the presiding judge.

The Judge's Goals

Like the lawyer who argues the case and the journalist who covers it, the individual sitting in judgment has a difficult two-part mission: first, and most important, to fulfill his or her professional duty as well as possible, and second, to protect and defend the work of the court. For judges, this mission is significantly more difficult than for either lawyers or journalists, because their role is not that of advocate, but of keeper and dispenser of justice.

A sitting judge's primary goal—the heart of the judicial agenda—is to ensure the fair and orderly administration of justice in the courtroom and to secure an equitable verdict in a systematic fashion. The judge is also at least partially responsible for maintaining the professional image of the judiciary. The code of conduct for federal judges outlines these principles in broad terms, stating, "A judge should be faithful to and maintain professional competence in the law, and should not be swayed by partisan interests, public clamor, or fear of criticism."[20] It goes on to say that a judge should "maintain order and decorum in all judicial proceedings,"[21] and should "be patient, dignified, respectful, and courteous to litigants, jurors, witnesses, lawyers and others with whom the judge deals in an official capacity."[22] In short, the judge must be all things to all people. Polite but powerful. Able to listen, but also to draw lines. Maintain the pose of dispassionate observer in a sea of turbulence and passion. Allow each side its say, while retaining ultimate control of the process. No surprise, then, to hear a judge say, "This is my courtroom."

Involvement with the Media

Some of the most challenging rulings a judge must issue involve more than guilt or innocence. Many judgments concern and affect the activities of the press or lawyers—limiting coverage of certain issues or preventing discussion of others, all to protect the character and credibility of the proceedings. Ultimately, a judge may be forced by one or both of these parties to punish violations, which in turn can lead to ensuing error or criticism.[23]

The judge's role is further complicated because he or she rarely addresses the media or the public directly, unlike lawyers who, barring a court order or the potential for prejudice to the case or client, may speak freely and frequently. Instead, judges must rely on interpretations by journalists—who frequently are not lawyers—of their generally technical rulings on everything from jury selection to press contact to the outcome of the case itself.[24] It is a delicate role that balances the public's right to know with the rights of the news media, the legal strategies of the lawyers, and the parties' rights to a fair trial.[25] This equilibrium is particularly difficult to maintain because the lawyers and journalists each feel they are the most important part of the process, and judges must try to achieve a constitutional balance.

Not everyone believes it is better for a judge to sit silently. Many journalists, particularly, believe judges should speak more often to the press and the public. As one leading legal journalist recently suggested to a group of newly appointed federal judges, they need to "do the kind of nuts-and-bolts explaining" of cases or procedures when a reporter calls.[26] Although the judicial community harbors skepticism about such a strategy, some judges clearly understand the benefits of this approach. At the U.S. Supreme Court recently, following the conclusion of a semiannual meeting of the Federal Judicial Conference (the policy-making body of the federal courts), the Chair of the Conference Executive Committee, Chief Judge Gilbert Merritt of the U.S. Court of Appeals for the Sixth Circuit, met with journalists to explain some of the Conference's votes. These included policy changes on issues such as cameras in courtrooms. Though the rulings did not involve rendering a verdict, the principle and benefits were the same. The media got their story in a timely fashion from an "inside" source, and the Conference was the beneficiary of accurate reporting.

Judges' roles, as well as the perception of judges, can change dramatically from one trial to the next, particularly with the occurrence of a recent high-profile trial or news coverage of a crime. For instance, the media inundation, the circus-like atmosphere, and probably the results of the O.J. Simpson criminal trial all contributed to a judicial order barring cameras in the civil trial, as well as a special order allowing closed-circuit television for a specific trial audience of victims' families. Similarly, erroneous reporting of the bombing in Atlanta during the 1996 Olympic Games probably contributed to a virtual information blackout to the press during the early stages of the Colorado murder investigation of six-year-old beauty pageant contestant, Jon Benet Ramsey. And new legal strategies—involving the rights of victims in a courtroom—are further changing the way a judge does business.[27]

Conclusion

The often adversarial and distrustful relationship between lawyers and journalists is sometimes warranted, frequently disproportionate as a result of misunderstanding, and usually avoidable. The two professions differ significantly; yet notwithstanding these conflicts—and perhaps because of them—the need for enlightened communication between lawyers and reporters has never been clearer. Given the substantial potential benefits to all parties, it would seem to be worth the effort.

Endnotes

1. One judge noted the "diabolically dangerous conceit" of each profession resulting from a mutual belief that each is the exclusive protector of the public interest. *See* Jack C. Doppelt, *Strained Relations: How Judges and Lawyers Perceive the Coverage of Legal Affairs,* 15 Just. Sys. J. 4190 (1991) (quoting Chief Judge Charles D. Breitell of the New York Court of Appeals).

2. *See* Mary Nell York, *Lawyers and the Media,* 3 Cal. Law. 62 (June 1983).

3. *See* Larry Reibstein & Daniel Klaidman, *The Wanna-be Hunt,* Newsweek, Aug. 12, 1996, at 22 (discussing identification of suspect in Olympic bombing).

4. Model Code of Professional Responsibility Canon 7 (1986).

5. Charles Williams, *Taking to the Airwaves Can Be Part of the Job,* Chi. Daily L. Bull., July 26, 1994, at 1.

6. Richard Cheney, *How Lawyers Can Polish Their Public Image by Knowing How to Deal with the Press, Media,* Nat'l L.J., Feb. 18, 1980, at 29.

7. Horace Greeley, *in* Home Book of Quotations 1602 (Burton Stevenson ed., 6th ed. 1949).

8. Laura Mansnerus, *Brash Publisher Is Leaving Behind His Legal Empire,* N.Y. Times, Mar. 3, 1997, at B1 (quoting former American Lawyer Media Chair, Steven Brill).

9. *See* Joseph Ungaro, *Lawyers and Reporters: A Media Perspective,* 69 Mich. Bar J. 816, 817 (1990).

10. There is another more formal way in which this education occurs. One recent project by *The Baltimore Sun,* for instance, has staffers at the daily newspaper volunteering in schools and publishing extra pages in the newspaper dedicated to combating illiteracy. *See* Lisa Bannon, *Should a Newspaper Be Teaching Kids to Read?,* Wall St. J., Apr. 1, 1988, at B1.

11. Oscar Wilde, *The Critic As Artist,* quoted in The Wit and Wisdom of Oscar Wilde, 128 (Alvin Redman ed, 1952).

12. Tom Wicker, On Press 179 (1975).

13. Henry Ward Beecher, *Proverbs from Plymouth Pulpit: The Press, in* HOME BOOK OF QUOTATIONS 1602 (Burton Stevenson ed., 6th ed. 1949).

14. A.J. LIEBLING, THE PRESS 6 (1964).

15. *See, e.g.,* Larry Sabato, FEEDING FRENZY: HOW ATTACK JOURNALISM HAS TRANSFORMED AMERICAN POLITICS (1991).

16. One informal survey, conducted before the 1997 civil trial of O.J. Simpson even began, found that at least 40 books had been written about the trial, the first 11 days after the bodies were discovered. Seventeen of those books made the *New York Times* bestseller list. The O.J. Simpson story was featured more than 20 times on the cover of the major news magazines, and at least 88 times on the cover of *The National Enquirer. See* Bill Carter, *Will the O.J. Case Still Sell?,* N.Y. TIMES, Feb. 6, 1997, at B11.

17. David A. Anderson, *Democracy and the Demystification of Courts: An Essay,* 14 REV. LITIG. 627 (1995).

18. *Id.* at 628–33.

19. *See* John Onion, *Mass Media's Impact on Litigation: A Judge's Perspective,* 14 REV. LITIG. 585, 589 (1995).

20. MODEL CODE OF JUDICIAL CONDUCT Canon 3A(1) (1986).

21. *See id.* Canon 3A(2).

22. *See id.* Canon 3A(3).

23. *See* Bruce Brown, *Judge Presses Counsel on Media Contact,* LEGAL TIMES, June 17, 1996, at 1, 6 (examining propriety of judge's request of lawyer to provide information about lawyer's business in context of lawyer's motion to recuse judge; judge interrogated lawyer about whether he was source for magazine article that offended judge, as result of comments made about him).

24. One New Jersey state judge who provided unpaid television commentary on various national legal issues was barred from continuing such activities because, officials asserted, the judge lent the prestige of his office to commercial ventures. Associated Press, *Judge Loses Court Appeal,* N.Y. TIMES, Mar. 18, 1997, at A25.

25. *See Panel Discussion: What to Do When Your Case Is Front-Page News,* 14 REV. LITIG. 595, 601 (1995) (comments by Professor Michael E. Tigar).

26. *See* Bruce Brown, *ABCs for Baby Judges,* LEGAL TIMES, June 10, 1996, at 6.

27. *See* Jeffrey Toobin, *Victim Power,* NEW YORKER, Mar. 31, 1997, at 40.

Media Rights and the Litigator **2**

Gregg D. Thomas[1]

MOST LAWYERS DEAL VERY RARELY with the news media. Even lawyers with busy litigation practices may go months or years without ever handling a case that garners the attention of journalists. Consequently, when a matter draws media scrutiny, most lawyers are unfamiliar with the legal issues that accompany press attention. This chapter presents a general introduction to those issues. Specifically, this chapter discusses (1) the rights of journalists (and the public generally) to attend judicial proceedings and to review court records, (2) the use of cameras in courtrooms, (3) media attempts to gain access to depositions, and (4) the privileges that apply when litigants attempt to obtain information from journalists.

Not surprisingly, the law relating to media matters varies greatly from one state to another. This chapter, therefore, contains only a broad discussion of select topics that commonly arise in "high-profile" cases. Lawyers who find themselves involved in such matters should research these issues more thoroughly before attempting to deal with media scrutiny.

Media Access to Judicial Proceedings

Lawyer-media conflicts seem to arise most often when litigants seek to close hearings or file court documents under seal. The problem becomes even more pronounced when lawyers try to close entire proceedings or entire case files. Media entities often are quite aggressive in asserting a First Amendment right to attend hearings and to review court papers. Consequently, access issues are a fertile ground for disputes between lawyers and the media.

The problem arises partly because lawyers have grown accustomed to stipulated protective orders that contain confidentiality provisions. Under the First Amendment, however, lawyers cannot simply stipulate to closure of courthouse files or courtroom doors. Even a showing of "good cause" is likely to be insufficient, as the public has First Amendment and common-law rights of access to judicial proceedings and records.

Common-Law Rights

The common-law right, the United States Supreme Court has found, reflects "the citizen's desire to keep a watchful eye on the workings of public agencies," including the courts and—when they are parties—other branches of government.[2] Courts reason that once parties bring a matter before a court for resolution, that case is no longer solely the parties' case, but also the public's case. Moreover, as the Court of Appeals for the Second Circuit has noted, "professional and public monitoring is an essential feature of democratic control."[3] Openness allows federal judges, appointed for life, "to have a measure of accountability and for the public to have confidence in the administration of justice."[4]

First Amendment Considerations

The First Amendment interest in open judicial records and proceedings serves similar goals. In *Richmond Newspapers, Inc. v. Virginia*, the Supreme Court stated that open trials are "an indispensable attribute" of our system of justice.[5] Consequently, "the right to attend criminal trials is implicit in the guarantees of the First Amendment."[6] Lower courts have extended this right to civil trials. Moreover, this right of access also applies to various pretrial proceedings and to documents. When the First Amendment right applies, the presumption of openness may be overcome only by an overriding interest based on findings that closure is essential to preserve higher values and is narrowly tailored to serve that interest. The public must receive notice and an opportunity to be heard on the issue, and findings in support of closure must be specific, so that a reviewing court can determine whether closure was proper.

Closure Rarely Granted

Given the judiciary's recognition of the importance of openness, even seemingly substantial interests will not always justify closure. For example, the United States Supreme Court has rejected as unconstitutional the idea that courtroom doors should always be closed during the testimony of a minor complainant in a sex-crimes case.[7] The invocation of the phrase "national security" likewise is no guarantee of broad closure.[8] Moreover, fair-trial concerns will justify only limited infringement of access rights, even when fair-trial rights already are strained by massive publicity.[9] Trade-secrecy claims also are likely to be scrutinized closely when advanced as a basis for closure, and concerns about juror privacy are rarely sufficient to overcome media access requests.[10]

These principles mean a litigator should stop and think before seeking closure of a hearing or court document. For example, a litigator should not expect reputational interests alone to justify closure—courts regularly reject closure arguments based upon a claim that public access will harm someone's reputation.[11] Also, cases concerning government will be particularly difficult to keep secret. When the government is a party or its activities are at stake, courts are particularly unlikely to close files and courtroom doors.[12] And do not expect closure of discovery to guarantee closure at trial; because the Supreme Court has repeatedly recognized a First Amendment right of access to court proceedings, trials are generally more difficult to conceal than discovery.[13]

Finally, in addition to these legal issues, consider the risk that asking for closure may do more to draw media attention than to prevent it. Because journalists are typically skeptical and inquisitive, you can expect a closure motion to draw attention from reporters even if the case so far has not garnered media scrutiny. Of course, to say that the media might question closure does not necessarily mean a formal access petition will be filed. In some cases, a lawyer seeking closure might head off an access fight by asking the court to seal only particular documents and by explaining to the media the nature of the information to be kept confidential. If a reporter knows the sealed documents discuss little more than the finer points of widget-making, the reporter is less likely to ask editors to call in the media lawyers than if an entire case file is sealed and no one will say why.

Cameras in the Courtroom

As the preceding section shows, the First Amendment and common-law rights of access to court proceedings and records have become well established in United States law. To say that journalists have access rights, however, does not mean that reporters can always bring recording equipment to court. The media have no constitutional right to televise trial proceedings. In fact, television cameras are forbidden in federal trial and appellate courts. The federal view, however, is a distinct minority. Some 47 states allow some form of television coverage of judicial proceedings. Therefore, lawyers who practice in state courts should be familiar with the rules that govern electronic-media access in their particular jurisdictions.

Varying State Standards

State courts apply widely varying standards in determining whether media should be allowed to cover a particular trial. For example, in Florida, the news media have a presumptive right to televise most trial proceedings, unless a party opposing coverage proves that cameras will have a substantial effect upon a particular witness, and that this effect will be qualitatively different from the effects of electronic media upon members of the public in general and of coverage by other types of media.[14] Other states, such as Ohio[15] and Tennessee,[16] recognize a presumption in favor of media access but allow trial courts discretion to decide whether particular trials may be televised. And some states, including Louisiana,[17] prohibit coverage of trial proceedings generally.

Just as jurisdictions vary in the rules they adopt, they also use different methods of adopting these rules. In a number of states, such as Alabama,[18] the applicable standards appear in the Canons of Judicial Ethics. In other jurisdictions, such as North Carolina,[19] the rules of procedure control. In some states, such as Virginia,[20] camera rules appear in state statutes. Finally, in jurisdictions such as Florida,[21] case law is key to understanding the electronic media's access rights. So a lawyer seeking guidance on camera issues may have to search in unexpected places to find controlling authority in a particular jurisdiction.

Despite this variety, the bottom line is that practitioners in just about every state face the possibility of camera coverage of court proceedings. Litigators in high-profile cases, therefore, should consider how cameras might affect those proceedings and should be familiar with applicable state standards for such coverage.

Media Access to Depositions

In addition to coverage of court proceedings, occasionally journalists have attempted to push their access rights beyond the courthouse door to include coverage of discovery. For example, some journalists have sought to attend depositions. Unfortunately, resolution of whether the media can attend depositions requires a state-by-state analysis—there is no one dispositive case. There are, however, general principles that offer the practitioner some guidance.

Guiding Principles

First, courts tend to keep civil depositions closed. In support of this decision, most courts cite the following language from *Seattle Times v. Rhinehart:*

Moreover, pretrial depositions and interrogatories are not public components of a civil trial. Such proceedings were not open to the public at common law . . . and, in general, they are conducted in private as a matter of modern practice. Much of the information that surfaces during discovery may be unrelated, or only tangentially related, to the underlying cause of action. Therefore, restraints placed on discovered, but not yet admitted, information are not a restriction on a traditionally public source of information.[22]

As this language indicates, other than the fact that civil pretrial matters have been traditionally closed, the reason for maintaining closure of civil depositions is that they routinely involve or identify information beyond the scope of that presented at trial. Accordingly, because media have the right of access to the trial, closure of the deposition does not violate any First Amendment rights.

Second—though this rule is not without exceptions—courts tend to keep discovery in criminal cases closed. In criminal cases, courts have reasoned, public access to discovery information at the moment it is first discovered presents hazards to other constitutional rights, because of uncertainty about the nature and content of the information. It is not possible beforehand to know, with any degree of certainty, what information will be discovered. Press attendance at depositions, it is feared, could injure the right to a fair trial, the privacy rights of both parties and nonparties, and the right to a trial in the venue of the alleged crime.

Third, in analyzing whether the media should be allowed access to civil or criminal depositions, some courts—most notably those in New York—have employed the following two-part test: whether the place and process have historically been open to the press and general public, and whether public access plays a significant positive role in the functioning of the particular process in question. The answers may determine the issue of access.[23]

The analysis does not end with whether the media can attend the deposition. Whether they may have access to deposition transcripts is yet another concern. Although courts seem willing to keep both criminal and civil depositions closed, they are reluctant to seal either criminal or civil deposition transcripts filed with the court. As discussed earlier in another context, the mere stipulation of the parties is usually insufficient to resolve the matter.[24]

Reporter's Privilege

Until now, this chapter has addressed matters arising when journalists seek information from the legal system. Occasionally, the opposite situation arises—that is, lawyers seek information from journalists. In many jurisdictions, judicially created or statutory privileges allow journalists to resist subpoenas that seek newsgathering information.

The Branzburg *Case*

The United States Supreme Court discussed the concept of a reporter's privilege in *Branzburg v. Hayes,*[25] and its companion cases, *In re Pappas* and *United States v. Caldwell.* In these cases, reporters refused to testify before grand juries concerning what they had personally observed and heard. The media advocated a broad First Amendment privilege that would apply to eyewitness accounts of crimes. The Court declined to recognize such a privilege; a plurality of four justices determined that no privilege existed for a reporter who was an eyewitness to a crime. However, the Court did not reject the reporter's privilege entirely. In a concurring opinion—the pivotal decision that created the *Branzburg* majority—Justice Powell wrote:

> I add this brief statement to emphasize what seems to me to be the limited nature of the Court's holding. The Court does not hold that newsmen, subpoenaed to testify before a grand jury, are without constitutional rights with respect to the gathering of news or in safeguarding their sources. . . . [A reporter's] asserted claim to privilege should be judged on its facts by the striking of a proper balance between freedom of the press and the obligation of all citizens to give relevant testimony with respect to criminal conduct. The balance of

these vital constitutional and societal interests on a case-by-case basis accords with the tried and traditional ways of adjudicating such questions.[26]

This pivotal opinion by Justice Powell, considered alongside four dissenters' opinions that also recognized a reporter's privilege, is the basis for most modern court opinions and statutes recognizing that privilege. For example, relying upon *Branzburg*, ten federal circuits have recognized a reporter's privilege based upon the First Amendment.[27] In addition to the constitutional qualified privilege, a similar privilege is recognized in many states by statute.[28]

Overcoming the Privilege

The privilege recognized by *Branzburg* and its progeny is not absolute. Though laws on the subject vary widely, a party seeking privileged news-gathering information typically can defeat application of the privilege by showing that (1) a compelling or heightened need for the information exists, (2) the information is relevant, and (3) the information is not available from alternative sources.[29] So, for example, when obvious possible alternative witnesses exist, they generally must be deposed or at least interviewed before an exhaustion claim will stand, even if that involves dozens or hundreds of depositions or interviews. Likewise, if a journalist's testimony is sought only for impeachment purposes, the privilege is likely to be upheld, on the theory that no compelling need exists.

The privilege is particularly difficult to overcome in civil cases. In criminal proceedings, the important constitutional rights possessed by criminal defendants present significant countervailing interests that weigh against the interest of the journalist in preventing disclosure. In civil discovery matters, however, the interest served by the unrestricted flow of public information protected by the First Amendment usually outweighs the subordinate interest served by the liberal discovery provisions embodied in the Federal Rules of Civil Procedure. Thus, in the ordinary case, the civil litigant's interest in disclosure should yield to the journalist's privilege.

However, the privilege may be inapplicable when, as in *Branzburg,* the journalist is an eyewitness to a crime or other event, such as an arrest. In fact, in some jurisdictions, the privilege protects only confidential sources.

Regardless of the scope of the privilege in a particular jurisdiction, however, a lawyer should expect considerable resistance from the media when news-gathering information is sought. Journalists oppose discovery of their work product because the public perception of media independence is compromised when reporters are converted into agents of litigants by their cooperation in an investigation, or by their submission to the state's subpoena power. Even when sources do not require confidentiality, they reasonably expect reporters to be independent. Subpoenas force reporters to breach this expectation and to testify against their sources. Reporters' credibility, therefore, suffers when reporters are compelled to serve as litigants' freelance investigators. Moreover, as a practical matter, trial subpoenas interfere with news gathering by leading to the sequestration of reporters. When journalists, who would otherwise be free to cover trials, are made witnesses, they are barred from those trials except when testifying. That is why any lawyer planning to seek discovery from the news media should expect considerable resistance when journalists are put in the unaccustomed role of being asked questions rather than asking them.

Endnotes

1. Portions of this chapter first appeared in Litigation, Vol. 24, No. 2, (Winter 1998), published by the ABA Section of Litigation.
2. Nixon v. Warner Communications, Inc., 435 U.S. 589, 597 (1978).
3. United States v. Amodeo, 71 F.3d 1044, 1048 (2d Cir. 1995).
4. *Id.*
5. Richmond Newspapers, Inc. v. Virginia, 448 U.S. 555, 569 (1980).
6. *Id.* at 580.
7. Globe Newspaper Co. v. Superior Court, 457 U.S. 596, 608 (1982); *see also* United States v. A.D., 28 F.3d 1353, 1360 (3d Cir. 1994) (rejecting theory that Federal Juvenile Delinquency Act requires closure of juvenile proceedings in all cases, and instead finding that "Congress left the difficult task of weighing the interests of the juvenile and the public to the informed discretion of the district judge in each case").

8. *See, e.g.,* United States v. Pelton, 696 F. Supp. 156, 159 (D. Md. 1986) (courtroom kept open throughout trial concerning delivery of national defense information to Soviet Union; when secret audio recordings were played through headphones for court, jurors, attorneys, and defendant, transcript was made available to public, only "very limited portions" redacted).

9. *See, e.g.,* United States v. McVeigh, 119 F.3d 806, 813–16 (10th Cir. 1997) (in Oklahoma City bombing case, hearings involving suppression, severance, and investigator's notes of interview with defendant were held in open court, and redacted versions of sealed documents were made available to public).

10. *See, e.g.,* SEC v. Stratton Oakmont, Inc., 24 Media L. Rptr. 2179, 1996 WL 312194, at *2 (D.D.C. June 5, 1996) (granting newspaper access to excerpts from court papers concerning United States Senator's dealings with brokerage firm, even though firm claimed release of court papers would disclose its "confidential practices and trade secrets").

11. *See, e.g.,* Publicker Industries v. Cohen, 733 F.2d 1059, 1074 (3d Cir. 1984) (presumption of openness was not overcome by "proprietary interest of present stockholders in not losing stock value or the interest of upper-level management in escaping embarrassment"); Brown & Williamson Tobacco Corp. v. FTC, 710 F.2d 1165, 1179 (6th Cir. 1983) (that release of information would harm company's reputation did not overcome public's right of access), *cert. denied,* 465 U.S. 1100 (1984); In re Continental Airlines, 150 B.R. 334, 340–41 (D. Del. 1993) (rejecting bankruptcy judge's decision to seal reviews of $68 million worth of accountants' and attorneys' fees and expenses; speculation that such reviews might contain defamatory material, the court found, did not overcome strong presumption in favor of access to judicial records).

12. *See, e.g.,* United States v. Beckham, 789 F.2d 401, 413 (6th Cir. 1986). ("when the conduct of public officials is at issue, the public's interest in the operation of government adds weight in the balance toward allowing" access); United States v. Gonzalez, 927 F. Supp. 768, 784 (D. Del. 1996) (noting "the absolute necessity of allowing the light of public scrutiny to shine brightly upon government agencies, the courts, and the judicial process, so that the citizenry may be fully informed").

13. *See, e.g.,* Richmond Newspapers, Inc. v. Virginia, 448 U.S. 555 (1980); *see also In re* Cincinnati Enquirer, 85 F.3d 255, 256 (6th Cir. 1996) ("It is contrary to centuries of Anglo-American jurisprudence to conduct jury trials in secret") (Merritt, J., considering emergency petition pursuant to Fed. R. App. P. 27); *In re* Application of CBS, Inc., 828 F.2d 958, 960–61 (2d Cir. 1987) (allowing media access to videotaped deposition introduced into evidence despite deponent's illness and claim of privacy).

14. *In re* Petition of Post-Newsweek Stations, Florida, Inc., 370 So. 2d 764 (Fla. 1979).

15. *See* Rule 12, Rules of Superintendence for the Courts of Ohio (1999).

16. *See* Tenn. Sup. Ct. R. 30 (1996).

17. *See* La. Code of Jud. Conduct, Canon 3(A)(9).

18. *See* Ala. Canons of Judicial Ethics, Canon 3(A)(7).

19. *See* N.C. Superior & Dist. Ct. R. of Practice 15 (1995).

20. *See* Va. Code Ann. § 19.2-266 (1999).

21. *See In re* Petition of Post-Newsweek Stations, Florida, Inc., 370 So. 2d 764 (Fla. 1979).

22. Seattle Times v. Rhinehart, 467 U.S. 20, 33 (1984).

23. *See, e.g.,* Scollo v. Good Samaritan Hosp., 175 A.D. 2d 278, 280, 572 N.Y.S.2d 730, 732 (App. Div. 1991); *see also* Estate of Rosenbaum v. New York City, 21 Media L. Rptr. 1987 (E.D.N.Y. Aug. 13, 1993) (Case No. 92-5414) (allowing news media representatives to attend deposition of mayor and former police commissioner).

24. *See* pages 21–22 *supra.*

25. Branzburg v. Hayes, 408 U.S. 665 (1972).

26. *Id.* at 708.

27. *See* United States v. LaRouche Campaign, 841 F.2d 1176 (1st Cir. 1988); United States v. Burke, 700 F.2d 70 (2d Cir.), *cert. denied,* 464 U.S. 816 (1983); United States v. Cuthbertson, 630 F.2d 139 (3d Cir. 1980), *cert. denied,* 449 U.S. 1126 (1981); LaRouche v. National Broadcasting Co., 780 F.2d 1134 (4th Cir.), *cert. denied,* 479 U.S. 818 (1986); Miller v. Transamerican Press, 621 F.2d 721 (5th Cir. 1980), *cert. denied,* 450 U.S. 1041 (1981); Cervantes v. Time, Inc., 464 F.2d 986 (8th Cir. 1972), *cert. denied,* 409 U.S. 1125 (1973); Farr v. Pitchess, 522 F.2d 464 (9th Cir. 1975), *cert. denied,* 427 U.S. 912 (1976); Silkwood v. Kerr-McGee Corp., 563 F.2d 433 (10th Cir. 1977); United States v. Caporale, 806 F.2d 1487 (11th Cir. 1986), *cert. denied,* 482 U.S. 917 (1987); Zerilli v. Smith, 656 F.2d 705 (D.C. Cir. 1981).

28. *See, e.g.,* D.C. CODE ANN. §§ 16-4701 to 16-4707 (1996); § 90.5015, FLA. STAT. (Supp. 1998); 735 ILL. COMP. STAT. §§ 5/8-901-909 (West 1992); IND. CODE ANN. §§ 34-3-5-1 (Michie 1992); NEB. REV. STAT. §§ 20-144 to 20-147 (1992); NEV. REV. STATE ANN. §§ 49.275, 49.385 (Michie 1986); OKLA. STAT. ANN. tit. 12, § 2506 (West 1996).

29. *See* notes 27–28 *supra.*

Fundamentals and Etiquette of Dealing with the Media 3

John E. Morris

To PARAPHRASE FREUD, "What *does* a reporter want?"

The short answer in my case would be this: A source like Buck Delventhal.

Buck was my boss in the San Francisco City Attorney's office. I used to sit in his office and marvel at how candidly he dealt with reporters. He was a 20-year veteran of the office at that point, and he headed the team that handled many of the city's most politically sensitive legal matters—constitutional challenges to ordinances and administrative decisions, opinions on the legality of legislative proposals, and the like; in short, grist for the City Hall reporters at the city's two daily papers and several neighborhood weeklies.

When I first worked for Buck, I would cringe as I listened to him on the phone—conceding that the other side had colorable arguments, or explaining the other side's arguments more clearly than it had in its briefs. Occasionally, he would even admit that the city had an uphill battle defending a law or some administrative decision. (He would explain that the City Attorney had a duty to defend the city, as long as it could do so in good faith.) Buck's approach went against everything I learned in five years as a litigator; in particular, the principle that you should always maintain the facade that your case is a "slam dunk" for your side. What astonished me most, though, was that those revealing statements never seemed to make it into print. Buck always came across in print as a neutral public servant doing his duty—a rather accurate picture.

Several years later, when I became a reporter, I began to understand why Buck fared so well with reporters. He was concise, clear, and candid. Reporters trusted and relied on him. And reporters go out of their way to treat sources like that fairly.

Fundamentals: Staying Out of Trouble

Lawyers' strategies for dealing with reporters vary with the nature of the story, the publication, and the reporter. Ongoing work with a reporter when a lawyer is involved in protracted litigation is very different from a one-time encounter with a journalist who knows nothing about the subject matter. Answering questions for a publication aimed at lawyers, such as *American Lawyer*, differs from speaking to a courthouse reporter for a local paper in a midsized city. Reporters' aims and sophistication, and their audiences, vary tremendously. And from my side, I value different sources for different reasons.[1]

Still, all reporters look for some basic things—the elements that help explain Buck's success: honesty, clarity, and politeness.

Be Honest

You can fool some reporters all the time, and all reporters some of the time. About once, generally. And heaven help you when you interact a second time with a reporter you misled. Reporters are unforgiving on this score. They will hold it against you, and they compare notes about people they do not trust.

Be Clear About What You Cannot Answer

The best way to avoid violating the first rule is to be clear about what you cannot (or choose not to) answer truthfully, and be ready to decline comment if you find yourself in danger of misleading a reporter. Reporters know how to handle a "no comment" response. They may not stop asking questions just because you say you cannot answer, but they understand the reply, particularly if it is expressed politely. (See Chapter 4 for more views on this issue.)

Be Polite

Politeness counts. Surprising as it may seem, reporters are not immune to courtesy. If I know someone will treat me professionally, I may be more likely to call back a second and third time to make sure I fully understand his or her side of a dispute, for instance. This is never more important than when a story criticizes you or your client. Often sources do not realize the effect their treatment of the reporter can have on the tone of the story. The reporters I know agonize about the impact of stories that are critical—particularly if they have been exposed to a subject's human side.

Good reporters strive to be fair even when the subject of a story has been uncooperative and belligerent. However, many reporters find it difficult to produce a balanced report if the subject acts that way, and there is a danger that reporters' views may be tainted by such treatment.

On the whole, I find that litigators are quite thick-skinned and not excessively defensive; they are accustomed to contentiousness and know how to respond to accusations and conflicting stories. Transactional lawyers, by contrast, are often more skittish and defensive about being interviewed.

Etiquette: Staying on the Reporter's Good Side

Remember That a Reporter Has a Deadline

I now have the luxury of working for a monthly magazine, but still I often must report stories at the last minute. Those who work at daily newspapers operate under very intense deadline pressure all the time. Like other reporters, I am annoyed by sources who do not return calls quickly when I have a deadline. By contrast, a spontaneous feeling of warmth wells up in me when people return calls quickly—or even when they have their secretaries call back to say when they will be available. I'm always impressed when a lawyer's secretary asks, "What's your deadline?" It tells me right away that this person is savvy, courteous, and attuned to the demands and requirements of my job.

Do Not Ignore Calls

Regardless of deadlines, sometimes returning the call *at all* is the issue.

Under some circumstances, you may not want to talk to a reporter and do not care if the story says, "James Smith did not return numerous calls placed to his residence, office, and cell phone, nor did he respond to several faxes sent to various locations." But in most cases, you are better off returning calls, even if only to say you cannot comment. Blatant evasion makes you the reporter's adversary—the quarry. If you are someone whose comment the reporter must seek (the lawyer for a defendant who has just been sued, for example), the reporter and his or her editors may be holding the story open past normal deadlines. Even if you cannot comment, a quick call to say so wins points with most reporters, including me.

Sometimes, even people who like to see their names in print do not return calls. I once met with a consultant who complained that our magazine does not quote experts from his firm frequently enough. The reason is simple: He is the head of the practice, and returns only about one call in five. If you are knowledgeable about a subject and are willing to be quoted as an expert, you should make a habit of returning calls consistently. It is a great way to make yourself a "go-to" source.

Understand That Reporters Want to Stay on the Record

Reporters interview people to get information, so I—like all reporters—assume that everything is on the record, for attribution, and can be quoted unless the source says otherwise. It is a reporter's nightmare to call a source with a follow-up question and be told, "Oh, I didn't mean for you to print that!" or, worse yet, "I never said that."

I am most comfortable dealing with sources who state clearly what is on the record and what is not. Journalists themselves may well differ in the terms they use. (See Chapter 5 for another journalist's view of "off the record.") However, the basic concepts are these:

- Fully on the record (comments attributed to you by name)
- Quotable, but not for attribution ("According to a lawyer who was involved in the settlement talks . . .")[2]
- On background (reporter can rely on your comments or use them to pursue a story but cannot attribute them in any way, even to an unnamed source)

Most litigators should have no problem with these concepts, because they are accustomed to speaking on the record (legally committing their clients to positions in the process) and going off the court record; yet I am surprised by how many are careless in dealing with reporters. I welcome those who want to establish explicit understandings at the beginning of our conversations. This is because I abhor misunderstandings about what was on the record and what was not. They create a dilemma for me. Of course, legitimate miscommunications can occur, and when that happens, I honor a source's request to correct a misunderstanding. But often the reason for a requested change is that the source had second thoughts about what he or she said on the record. Protecting people with such regrets is not my job.

Those who do have second thoughts about something they said should simply ask the reporter not to repeat it, rather than denying they ever said it at all. A lawyer I had interviewed many times (who was always helpful and candid) once called me after one of our fact checkers called him to verify a particularly witty quote.[3] "I know I said it, John," he said, "I just wondered if you could see your way to leaving my name off it." How could I refuse? The comment was attributed to an unnamed defense lawyer familiar with the case. That will not work every time, but reporters value good sources and do not like to antagonize them. You should bear that in mind if you think a reporter will need to deal with you again.

Pithiness Counts

"Why can't I ever get a 'yes' or a 'no' out of you lawyers," Craig Matters, an editor of mine, once barked in exasperation after enduring a lengthy discourse in response to a seemingly simple question. His point was well taken. The longer I—as a reporter— deal with lawyers, the more I notice how many of them cannot get to the point. I recently called a lawyer to verify a two-word term of art in antitrust law. My question required a simple "yes" or "no" response, but it took 15 minutes to confirm that my understanding was correct.

The issue is not just about wasted time. Often I finish a long interview only to find that I do not have one good direct quote—I need to paraphrase the lawyer because nothing was stated directly. Usually the problem concerns an obsession with minutiae that are of no interest to anyone except the lawyers involved in the case. But in journalism—even print journalism—the sound bite rules. Assuming you want to see your name in print (or get across your client's side of the story), you should try to get to the bottom line when talking with reporters. Think of it from the reporter's perspective. Yes, you may have devoted the last few years of your life to a 13-count, 400,000-pages-of-discovery lawsuit, which has been up to the court of appeals twice, but the reporter must summarize the matter in a paragraph. Have some sympathy by getting to the point as quickly as possible.

He who speaketh pithily will be rewarded with quotes. You need not have Oscar Wilde's wit; I—like most reporters—will settle for a clear and concise statement of your side's position. Many litigators are good at this, because the same skill is invaluable in writing briefs and arguing cases in court. But far too many still need to hone the skill.

Color Helps

Nevertheless, it is also true that colorful quotes are better than merely pithy ones. A good metaphor or a sarcastic characterization—those give stories zing. I go out of my way to work in a good quote, even if not central to the story, and I return to sources who are clever.

Several years ago, while scouting a potential profile of Bill Shernoff, a California plaintiff's lawyer who specialized in insurance bad-faith suits, I interviewed Weaver Gaines, the former general counsel of Mutual Life Insurance Company of New York, who knew Shernoff and respected his ability to select strong cases. "When you learned Shernoff had one of your cases, you started looking for the problem," Gaines said, "like a claims agent who said, 'I don't care if your daughter spends the rest of her life like a garden snail.'" I vowed right then that I would write the profile—so I could use the quote, if for no other reason. One caveat: A lawyer who worked on a case I covered for more than a year could always be counted on for a lively—and usually sarcastic—quote about the other side. The problem was that the same quotes frequently appeared in rival papers. I, along with most reporters, resent being given canned pithy quotes that are also offered to the competition.

The Value of Long-Term Sources

The considerations discussed above apply to all types of stories. But I have many different kinds of relationships with different sources. Writing a story on a daily deadline, when I must talk with people I have not previously interviewed, is quite different from working on a feature about a subject I have covered in the past, when I know many of the sources well. The people with whom I have worked over time are the ones I value most as sources, and the ones I most enjoy. The experience is much more rewarding, and safer—for both me and the sources—if we trust each other.

Among my long-term sources, I look for more than just honesty and an understanding of journalism ground rules. I look for people who are insightful, willing to share information, and balanced in their views, and whose motives are not self-serving—or at least not blatantly so. The most knowledgeable people in any field are often the most enthusiastic about the subject, and many feel strongly that their individual fields deserve attention in the press. One need not be a publicity hound to like talking with reporters.

Good instincts for stories is also a plus. For example, it was an insurance defense lawyer who suggested that I profile Shernoff, the bad-faith specialist. My source said that Shernoff had compiled a tremendous record suing insurers, but was not well known outside the industry. The defense lawyer said his adversary was particularly remarkable because he was liked by the defense bar. His instinct for a profile of someone who was not a stereotype was perfect, and resulted in a good story.

Approaches to Avoid

Certain approaches to interacting with reporters typically result in soured relationships. Following are a few of those that lawyers should avoid.

Do Not Use Heavy-Handed Tactics: They Often Backfire

Litigators and other lawyers are in the business of trying to control those who have interests adverse to their clients. Those instincts can be dangerous when dealing with reporters. Lawyers should not view the reporter-source relationship as they would a relationship with opposing counsel. The reporter cannot subpoena documents or compel testimony, and the lawyer cannot threaten the reporter with sanctions, or expect the reporter to take bullying in stride the way a courtroom adversary might.

A case in point: Early in my career as a reporter, I had a lead on a story about a law firm that employed nonlawyer "cappers" on commission to bring in cases. The firm was also alleged to have paid kickbacks to union officials for case referrals. The partners I tried to interview would not talk to me on the phone, but offered to be interviewed in their offices. When I arrived, I was ushered into a conference room where I was greeted by eight lawyers—seven lawyers from the firm and a criminal defense lawyer—and a court reporter. The chair next to the court reporter was reserved for me. I spent three hours in an eight-on-one interrogation. Many months later—after repeated threats of suit and state bar complaints against me, consultations with libel lawyers, and dozens of faxes—the story ran. Needless to say, the message the firm conveyed was that it had something to hide. Although these kinds of tactics might intimidate some reporters and publishers, my editors stood behind me, and the tactics only made me more keen to nail down the story.

Even lawyers who can contain their desires to bully reporters should be careful that their instincts to bludgeon the opposition do not get the better of them in other ways. For example, in a case that appeared on the front of *The Wall Street Journal* in 1996,[4] a tobacco company's lawyers fed investigators' reports and documents to two reporters working on a profile of a whistleblower. The reporters were amazed at the array of supposed misdeeds by the ex-employee that the company unearthed, and they began checking the information. The story, which the company hoped would taint the ex-employee, instead was a brilliant debunking of a misguided smear campaign by the company based on a sloppy investigation and the misreading of documents.

Refrain from Speculation

Speculation has its place. It may suggest avenues of reporting, for instance. But occasionally sources portray things in exaggerated terms without indicating that they are speculating or being hyperbolic. Recently, I had a series of long conversations on background with a litigator at a major law firm. He said he could not go on the record, but he passed along some fascinating pieces of information about a story I was reporting, including the "fact" that a key document was signed by someone who would not normally have signed it because other lawyers refused to sign it. I tried to confirm this from other sources and could not. When I called the original source again, he explained he simply *inferred* that the normal people did not sign the document because there was an internal dispute on their side. Needless to say, I prefer sources who distinguish fact from fiction. I will know in the future to take what this source says with a grain of salt.

Do Not Play Games "Off the Record"

Reporters often are too quick to let people talk on background or not for attribution. We should probably hold people responsible for their statements more often than we do. But few things are more frustrating for a reporter than a source who reveals unverifiable information on background that contradicts what everyone else tells the reporter, particularly if the source's assertions are self-serving.

For instance, the managing partner of a firm once wrote me a two-page, single-spaced letter marked, "Confidential—Off The Record" (a bit strange in itself), defending his firm against some charges of impropriety. The problem was that none of his assertions could be checked, and I had a lot of on-the-record information from other sources supporting the allegations. I felt he was just trying to trick me into omitting parts of my story.

On my best days I fight to keep sources on the record. But I will let people explain their views on background—particularly if I have reason to believe they may have some obligation not to disclose important facts that bear on the story. For example, someone may be able to tell me on background something that I can independently verify and that explains a decision or event that otherwise looks strange or improper. But if the source gives nothing I can check and I have other reasons to doubt his or her account, I may just conclude that he or she is trying to take advantage of me—particularly if the spin being put on facts is self-serving.

Do Not Expect Quid Pro Quo Treatment: It Offends Most Reporters

Occasionally sources hint broadly, or say outright, that they expect something in return for their help—usually some favorable publicity. I know the game may be played this way at some publications, but I—along with many other reporters—feel insulted when sources request such treatment.

Do Not Ask Reporters Whether You Will Like the Story

I am not sure why this question annoys me so; perhaps because it is not the issue. The truth is—and this is my response to the question—I never can tell. I feared that the subject of a profile I wrote several years ago would be unhappy because it alluded to some sexual harassment complaints against him. Two days after the story ran, he had his firm's librarian order 20 copies. Evidently it was good enough for all the family to read. Conversely, I have written stories I thought were flattering to people, only to have them become upset because of some minor part of the story that, in their eyes, tainted the entire picture.

My goal is to write a fair and balanced story, and let the chips fall where they may. Asking me to predict reactions calls for speculation. I will instruct myself not to answer that question.

Endnotes

1. I dislike the word "source" because it conjures up images of Bob Woodward and Carl Bernstein in some darkened parking lot. But it is a universal term of art among reporters, applied to anyone to whom they talk for a story.

2. Our company requires reporters to provide some information about unnamed sources—usually something about the basis of their knowledge or their allegiances (for example, "a lawyer who attended the meeting" or "a lawyer with ties to the defendant"). We are prohibited from saying, "Sources say. . . ."

3. Our fact checkers do not read back quotes verbatim, they paraphrase them so they verify the substance of the remark. In this case, it was the thrust of the quote—not the precise wording—that was a problem.

4. Suein L. Hwang & Milo Geyelin, *Getting Personal: Brown & Williamson Has 500-Page Dossier Attacking Chief Critic,* WALL ST. J., Feb. 1, 1996, at A1.

Ground Rules for Communication

4

Gail Appleson

IN THE EARLY 1990S, a spokesperson for a cigarette company complained that one of my stories unfairly focused on comments by plaintiffs' lawyers suing the tobacco industry. When I noted that I had called his company as well as others for a response but no in-house or outside counsel would talk to me, he could only sigh and admit the difficulty of his job. The spokesperson agreed that tobacco lawyers rarely talked to the press, making it very difficult for the media to present any kind of defense to allegations of deceptive behavior.

Although tobacco lawyers have become more accessible over the years, the tension between journalists and cigarette companies is a dramatic example of what happens when one side of a controversy declines to speak to the media. Responsible reporters with important stories based on reliable information or sources are going to write them, with or without lawyers' help. That is our time-honored responsibility—to disseminate news. Your responsibility as a lawyer, of course, is to your client. The question, then, is whether you help your client by helping a journalist to report accurately. I believe that every honest party benefits from clear and fair reporting.

To Speak or Not to Speak

Unfortunately, many lawyers view the world of communications like a criminal trial. They believe their clients will be considered innocent unless proven guilty beyond a reasonable doubt. They may decide that more harm will be done by speaking—much like letting a defendant take the stand—than by keeping quiet.

In the arena of public opinion, however, silence can be deadly. Lawyers' refusals to comment can appear suspicious. If accusations are false, then explanations can often help—not harm—clients. Refusing to respond can also make lawyers seem indifferent to the public's welfare, and even arrogant, as though they believe they (and their clients) are above the law.

Many crisis managers probably will tell you the same thing. For example, Gerald C. Meyers, former Chair of American Motors, warns against the "no comment" stance. "The day of 'no comment' is past. With the public as informed as it is today, those words are interpreted as a confession of guilt," Meyers writes.[1]

Meyers discusses the problems a chief executive officer faces when a scandal hits the company. Meyers says the company's public relations person will usually counsel openness: "Deal with the issue forthrightly and the fuss will be over quickly. Retreating behind a stone wall will only raise suspicions that more lurid misdeeds remain to be discovered."[2] Meyers writes that in-house counsel will likely advise an opposite tack: "Decline comment, . . . and save everything for the battle in the courtroom or the privacy of negotiations. Smart executives are not intimidated by lawyers who don't have to run the business once the legal skirmishing is over. Trying to minimize or hush up an event can do just the opposite, blowing it up to major proportions in the public's mind."[3]

Concerns When Deciding to Speak

Even lawyers who agree that speaking to the media is in their clients' best interests are frequently concerned about being quoted accurately, and fear that their comments will be taken out of context. Marcia Horowitz, an executive vice president at the New York public relations firm of Rubenstein Associates, has advised law firm clients for many years. She believes it is unusual for this concern to become a reality. "I have found it is rare that lawyers complain that they have been misquoted,"[4] she says. She also believes that the relationship between lawyers and reporters has become much less adversarial over the past few years: "Most of the time reporters appreciate lawyers helping them, especially when they are on deadline and need to be brought up to speed quickly on the subject matter."[5]

Of course, there is no way to guarantee that a story will be completely accurate, short of allowing the lawyer being quoted to read the piece before it is published. Almost never—except in the rarest of situations—will reporters agree to this. But there are many ways that lawyers and reporters can work together to make sure they understand each other. As with any other type of relationship, it is important that both lawyer and journalist approach their conversations with a certain respect for each other's job, skills, and time pressures. Other chapters discuss these matters in more detail, but a couple of issues merit repetition here.

Just as a reporter must understand that a lawyer is taking time away from a busy practice to explain issues or make comments for a story, a lawyer should realize that a journalist usually has a very short period—often a matter of hours—to compile information and write a simplified story on a complex matter. Therefore, lawyers should understand that reporters are not necessarily being combative in the way they ask questions—they are trying to understand the bottom line quickly. Keeping this in mind can ward off many misunderstandings from the very beginning.

Indulging in legalese, giving vague and evasive explanations, and talking down to reporters will only make a difficult situation worse. Once a lawyer agrees to speak to the media, he or she should be as clear and straightforward as possible.

Because reporters are often thrown into stories cold, they may have had little time to research a topic, particularly if it involves breaking news. Although you would expect a "beat" reporter who has been covering an area for some time to be knowledgeable, you should not assume that a general assignment reporter is irresponsible or lazy because he or she is unfamiliar with you, your case, or your area of specialization.

Establishing Ground Rules

In a perfect world, reporters and lawyers would have time to meet in person and get to know each other before a story breaks. But realistically, most conversations between the two take place on a deadline, and both parties must, to a great extent, rely on telephone skills to establish rapport.

I find it best if both parties agree on ground rules *before* an interview takes place—not at the end or even after the first few sentences are uttered. Journalists generally agree that once an interviewee starts talking and knows the comments might be published, there is no going back. If you make your comments and then throw in at the end, "This is off the record, right?," do not be surprised if the reporter gives you a firm "No."

Agree on Definitions

When discussing ground rules, it is wise to make sure both parties agree on definitions. For example, "off the record" can mean many things to different people. Some reporters think it means they can use your comments without attribution or by attributing them to a source. If you do not want your comments published in any form, you must make that clear at the beginning of your conversation and tell the reporter you are speaking only on background, to help him or her understand the issue. At that point, a reporter may not want to proceed, which will save both of you time and misunderstandings. If you agree to let your comments be used, but you do not want to be named, you should also discuss how the reporter will attribute the quotes. The journalist may have some description in mind that might identify you.

Discuss Tape Recording

You might also wish to discuss whether the reporter plans to tape the conversation. I try to use a tape recorder whenever possible, regardless of the length of the conversation or whether it is on the phone or in person. This is the best way to ensure the accuracy of quotes. If you have an off-the-record conversation or discuss something that could come back to haunt you, you may want to make sure it is not recorded. This should be made clear to the reporter ahead of time.

The Importance of Time

As has been noted previously, and will be noted again, time constraints rule in the journalism business. When talking to reporters, particularly those working for daily publications, keep in mind that they are working under tight deadlines—a return telephone call late in the day may do little or no good. Reporters working for daily morning newspapers generally must submit their stories by 5:00 or 6:00 P.M. Although there is another deadline at 9:00 or 10:00 P.M., this is usually reserved for major late-breaking stories. Even if your comment gets in after the first deadline, it may not make all editions of the paper.

Journalists working for competing wire services are often timed against each other on important stories, so speed is especially essential for them. It is often through the wires that other media learn about an event. If you are prompt in responding to a call for information, your name may be the one gaining the most exposure. In addition, although a wire story may be updated throughout the day and night, keep in mind that the wire service's clients include newspapers and television stations. Therefore, getting back to a wire reporter many hours after an event has occurred may be as useless as missing a newspaper deadline.

Finally, because reporters of all types usually have a word or line limit, if you call late they may have already spoken with enough sources to fill their story.

Using Public Relations Specialists

Due to the possibility of misunderstandings about these conventions, lawyers and reporters should try to build bridges whenever possible before that last-minute story breaks. One method of doing this is through public relations specialists. Although reporters often bristle when dealing with an intermediary, a well-informed public relations person often can be a priceless go-between.

"Well-informed" is the key adjective here. An effective public relations agent must know the lawyer's area of expertise and articulation skills, as well as the journalist's beat and reporting abilities. Few things are more annoying to a reporter than a cold call from a public relations person who pitches a story or client that is totally inappropriate to that journalist's audience, or that has absolutely no news value. For example, there are about ten reporters from different news organizations in the courthouse pressroom where I work. Although many of us write for very different audiences, it is common to hear each of our phones ring one after another. You can tell from the conversations or answering machines that the calls are from the same public relations person pitching the same story with absolutely no regard for whom we write. A friend in the public relations business told me this technique is called, "spray and pray." Reporters grimace and complain to each other about the annoyance and brand the caller as a pest. Unfortunately, that feeling sometimes gets extended to the client as well.

On the other hand, an agent who can spot an important breaking story or trend—and lead the appropriate lawyer to the journalist—is a gem. And if that reporter needs an explanation in a big hurry and a public relations person can quickly find the right lawyer, well then it's a marriage made in heaven, as they say. Those lawyers and that public relations person will definitely make it to the reporter's Rolodex. That also means the public relations person will probably have success connecting the reporter to other lawyers at a particular firm.

A public relations person can also help assure the lawyer that a reporter has a good reputation and her or his writing has been fair and accurate, which leads to smoother communications with the media. A noteworthy example of this occurred with Jones, Day, Reavis & Pogue, a law firm that has established a reputation among reporters as being open and media-friendly. (Jones Day uses the public relations firm Dix & Eaton in its home base of Cleveland, as well as individual specialists in other cities.) I know that if I need an articulate lawyer to help me in a hurry, I can count on Jones Day, unless the firm has a conflict with the subject matter of my story. Because of this, my Rolodex is filled with Jones Day lawyers with whom I have built relationships over the years.

In-house public relations persons can bring about some of the same positive relationships, although they are generally far less aggressive than outside firms. The in-house public relations specialist is particularly important in arranging meetings between reporters and partners to discuss general topics that may lead to future stories.

The need for effective public relations can rapidly turn from a luxury into a necessity when lawyers are involved in high-profile cases. A lawyer or law firm can quickly be deluged with continuing calls from reporters when a big story breaks, and it may be impossible to get back to everyone. In this situation, lawyers sometimes choose to call back only certain reporters or those from a limited number of news organizations. This route can expose lawyers to anger from reporters or media outlets that have been ignored. Do not forget that news organizations monitor each other's output, and that reporters from different organizations *do* talk to each other. In situations too big for one lawyer to handle, you probably should consider appointing a spokesperson or public relations firm to help. Although reporters always prefer to get information straight from the lawyer, a public relations person may be needed to make sure the information gets disseminated as expeditiously and fairly as possible.

Drexel, Burnham Lambert Inc.'s bankruptcy filing on Valentine's Day in 1990 is a perfect example. Here was one of the most powerful investment bankers of the high-flying eighties forced into Chapter 11 after pleading guilty to securities fraud and watching the junk-bond market collapse. Drexel's name was synonymous with financial wizard Michael Milken, who pioneered the use of high-risk, high-yield bonds to finance megamergers. The New York firm of Weil, Gotshal & Manges, which represented the debtor Drexel, was flooded with calls—many from reporters who had never before covered a bankruptcy and who wanted quick explanations of mind-boggling complexities. Alan Miller, one of the Weil Gotshal partners handling the bankruptcy, says that Drexel's then-in-house public relations chief, Steven Anreder, devised some very useful strategies.

One that worked very well, according to almost everyone involved, was hosting off-the-record briefings for reporters covering the Drexel bankruptcy. During these sessions, held in a Weil Gotshal conference room, Miller and other lawyers walked reporters through the complex proceeding. Reporters were allowed to ask questions and develop rapport with lawyers involved in the case. Although the briefings were "off-the-record," journalists were allowed to report information from the sessions if the Weil Gotshal lawyers first checked the accounts for accuracy. According to Anreder (who now has his own public relations business), the sessions were like tutorials, and freed everyone from the concern that statements would be taken out of context.

Endnotes

1. Gerald C. Meyers, When It Hits the Fan—Managing the Nine Crises of Business 236 (1986).
2. *Id.* at 46.
3. *Id.*
4. Interview with Marcia Horowitz, December 2, 1999.
5. *Id.*

"Off-the-Record" versus "On-the-Record" Comments

5

Alan Abrahamson

Picture THIS: After years as a deputy in the public defender's office, you have finally hung your own shingle. One morning, you settle in at your desk, shuffle the morning paper, and see—right there in black and white on the front page—the gory details of an autopsy report a judge had ordered sealed. The report incriminates your client. The newspaper story says the report was "obtained" from "a source familiar with the case."

Or imagine this: You are a real estate lawyer. The morning paper spills forth the details of the mayor's new policy initiative. If enacted, it will derail that big deal you are crafting. The details of the initiative, obviously leaked to influence debate at City Hall, are attributed to a "senior aide who requested anonymity."

"On" or "Off" the Record?

Scenes like these happen every day in newspapers and towns across America. They highlight the importance to the news business of comments or docu-

51

ments obtained either "on the record" or "off the record." It is absolutely imperative to understand the difference between the two. It is also critical to comprehend that among journalists and their sources, there are various shades of both.

Fortunately, it is all very easy to understand. So easy, in fact, that it is one of the very first things taught in journalism school. It is one-third of a veritable journalism trinity—the others being, "Spell everything correctly," and "Never, ever make anything up." It is also quite easy to put into practice by you—the source.

The Basic Rule

The starting place is this basic rule:

> *Everything is on the record unless both parties to the conversation agree that it is not.*

Suppose you are prosecuting a hard-fought murder trial. Walking out of the courtroom one day after a particularly grueling session, reporters in tow, you mutter to no one in particular, "That judge is a real donkey." The next morning's headlines bleat: "Lawyer Calls Judge an Ass." Even if you mutter under your breath, you are on the record. And if you take that thought to its logical conclusion, this much should be obvious: reporters are particularly interested in comments made under one's breath, for they often reveal what a source is really thinking.

The Qualifier

Like most rules, the basic rule comes with a qualifier. This is it:

> *You can agree to make something off the record only if you do so before you make the comment.*

The lawyer muttering about the judge realizes 15 minutes later that the judge is unlikely to regard being compared to a donkey as a compliment. Back in the office, the lawyer calls the reporter and says, "You can't use that comment you heard me say about the judge. It's off the record." The reporter responds, "No, it's not; and I can indeed use it if I want." According to the ethics of journalism (no smart remarks here, please), the reporter is right.

But Should the Reporter Remove the Comment Nevertheless?

Here is where things get interesting, however. Without question, the reporter is perfectly within his or her bounds to say, "Read it in the paper and weep." Some reporters have been known to do just that. But other reporters prefer an approach that doesn't so much resemble General Sherman marching through Atlanta. They hew to a George Bush-like "kindlier, gentler" school. Telling a source to "read it and weep" is not likely to foster the kind of relationship a reporter needs when covering an ongoing story, particularly a high-profile one. With such a story, it is usually in everyone's interest to go along and get along. And in such a situation, the reporter must weigh whether to honor the request to take the comment out of the story.

Such a decision involves a slew of variables:

♦ How important is a friendly and nonadversarial relationship with the lawyer who made the remark?

♦ How important is the remark to the day's story?

♦ How important is it to the continuing saga of the trial?

♦ How prominently have editors decided the story will be played (in a paper, for example, in what section and page will it appear and what size headline will it get)?

♦ What time is it in the day, and how much time until deadline?

As a general proposition, the later the time, the more difficult it is to convince editors to make a change in a story. What time is too late? Because deadlines vary considerably, you should learn those that apply to your local media. At one newspaper, for example, the first deadline for the daily paper is 5:00 P.M., and the final deadline is 10:00 P.M. Stories that will run in the weekend editions of the paper (here, "weekend" means the Sunday and Monday papers) are supposed to be filed by the prior Thursday. It is not uncommon, however, for them to be filed on the prior Friday.

Personally, I have never burned a source who asked for forbearance. It is more important to me to continue relationships with the lawyers involved.

The Supreme Court Case:
Cohen v. Cowles Media Co.

Make no mistake: from a newspaper perspective, this is a complicated issue. And a 1991 U.S. Supreme Court ruling made it even more complex. In *Cohen v. Cowles Media Co.*,[1] the Court ruled that the First Amendment does not protect a news organization from a lawsuit if it promises to keep the name of a source secret, but later discloses it. The case concerned a peculiar situation. In most instances, news organizations go to court to protect the confidentiality of their sources. In this case, though, two newspapers were put in the position of defending a decision to disclose the identity of a source over his objections. In the midst of the 1982 election campaign in Minnesota, Republican activist Dan Cohen offered reporters from various news organizations documents that would embarrass the Democratic candidate for lieutenant governor. Marlene Johnson, the Democratic candidate, had been arrested for "unlawful assembly" during a 1969 protest rally and for a $6.00 shoplifting charge in 1970. The 1969 case was eventually dismissed; the shoplifting charge led to a conviction that eventually was vacated.

Cohen insisted that his name not be used. Reporters for the *Minneapolis Star Tribune,* the *St. Paul Pioneer Press,* the Associated Press, and WCCO-TV agreed and were given the documents. Their editors promptly confronted this dilemma: If they reported only the damaging documents, they would be allowing the Republicans to deal a last-minute blow to the Democrats. If they did not report them, they could be accused of engaging in a cover-up that shielded the Democrats. Editors of the two newspapers chose to publish the documents, but also to disclose that Cohen was the source. In both instances, the papers ignored their customary policy and overruled the wishes of their reporters. The Associated Press reported the story without mentioning the source. WCCO-TV chose not to report anything.

When his name appeared in print, Cohen was fired from his public relations job. He then sued the papers, charging they had breached a contract. A jury agreed and awarded him damages. The Minnesota Supreme Court, however, tossed out the award, saying the First Amendment's guarantee of a free press protects newspapers from lawsuits of this sort. A divided U.S. Supreme Court took a different view. Writing for a five-to-four majority, Justice Byron White rejected the notion that the press has an absolute constitutional right to publish any information it chooses about a newsworthy event, as long as it is truthful. Instead, he said, state courts may enforce laws that "simply require those making promises to keep them."[2]

Not surprisingly, lawyers who represent the news media have generally criticized the decision, calling it a dangerous development; they fret that if a source simply does not like an article, he or she will sue. Reporters, meanwhile, have been reminded that they too are bound by the notion of promissory estoppel—even if most newspeople have no idea what that phrase means.

The Bottom Line: What Should You Do?

So what does it all mean for you? The Supreme Court opinion, the basic rule of "off the record," and the qualifier—what does it mean in day-to-day practice? It means this: You must be sophisticated. You must know how to go "off the record" with a reporter. And you must know that "off the record" can have different meanings. Therefore, you must specify your desired context. Essentially, there are three permutations:

1. It can mean, "You, the reporter, may not print the quote."
2. It can mean, "You, the reporter, may print the quote but not attribute it to me." (This produces the gauzy kind of attribution we often see, such as, "A source familiar with the legal team said . . .")
3. It also could very well mean, "You, the reporter, may not print the quote or my name or identify me in any way, but

you may use the information I am giving you to investigate or confirm what I am saying."

Negotiate a Mutual Understanding, or Don't Talk

Most people unfamiliar with "off the record" assume it means Number 1. However, reporters and those who deal frequently with the media most commonly find themselves in situations Number 2 and Number 3. Whichever the situation, before you begin speaking substantively off the record, negotiate first with the reporter a mutual understanding of what it means.

When negotiating, it does not matter what you call the material: "off the record," "background," "not for attribution," or any other term. Whatever you call it, make sure you and the reporter have the same understanding of how it will be used. Do it before you begin talking. This is not difficult. You are all lawyers. This is what you are trained to do. Also, and this may come as a shock or a delightful surprise, but in such a negotiation, you—the source— hold the power. The reporter can cajole and wheedle and plead and beg. It is still up to you to decide the conditions under which your words will be used, if at all. Can't get the deal you want? Then don't talk.

Though "not for attribution" and "background" can mean different things to different people, in general the phrases have a commonly understood meaning. "Not for attribution" is situation Number 2. Attributing vital information to reliable and well-placed but unnamed sources is an honored journalistic tradition. "Background" is situation Number 3. If both reporter and source agree on Number 2, that situation typically demands one more negotiation before the substantive talking begins: how the source is to be identified in print. Is it "senior aide?" A "law enforcement source?" A "source familiar with the investigation?" In hammering out what to call the source in print, the reporter is obliged, for purposes of credibility, to be as precise as possible with the identification. Yet the reporter also must take great care to disguise the speaker's identity; often, careers and money are on the line, and sometimes even lives.

Other Considerations

As noted in one of the better journalism textbooks, *Investigative Reporting*,[3] some editors—and a great many people not in the news business—argue that if a source wants to criticize some other person or institution, then he or she should stand tall and reveal his or her identity. Some situations would absolutely seem to demand attributed quotes. Years before the Supreme Court's opinion in *Cohen,* for example, I learned that the better practice in a heated campaign was to attribute politically sensitive charges to a named source. Other situations demand at least identification of the ax the source is grinding; that is, which side of the issue or argument he or she takes. Yet many reporters believe that relying on unnamed sources is an investigative reporting technique of real merit. Ask Woodward and Bernstein.

Why do reporters care about using sources "on background" (Number 3)? Because it is an invaluable reporting tool. According to *Investigative Reporting,* many otherwise reluctant sources can be approached and successfully interviewed if the information they provide is on an off-the-record or not-for-attribution basis.[4] An off-the-record interview can provide valuable leads; it also allows a reporter to ask other sources the same question on the record that was asked of a first source off the record. The second time around, the questions will often be more pointed because the reporter already will know a lot of the answers. Plus, the reporter is in a much stronger position to dig for other answers.

Sometimes, a source will go on and off the record, back and forth, a dozen or more times in a conversation. It's hard for the reporter—let alone the source—to know what is usable and what is not. This really does happen. When it does, the better practice is for the reporter to review the conversation with the source before they part. That way, there is no misunderstanding.

As a source, you do not have the right to have a story read to you before it is reported. You do, however, have the right to condition your interview on the reporter's agreement to read back quotes to you. You also are within bounds to make certain the reporter understands completely the context in which those quotes were made, and ought to appear in print.

A Final Rule

This leads to a logical conclusion and a final rule:

Deal with reporters you trust.

Give everyone a chance. But, like a barrel of apples, every bunch of reporters includes good and bad. Establish ongoing relationships with those who earn your confidence and always, always return their phone calls before deadline—that is the cardinal rule in getting along with a reporter.

Endnotes

1. Cohen v. Cowles Media Co., 501 U.S. 663 (1991).
2. *Id.* at 671.
3. DAVID ANDERSON & PETER BENJAMINSON, INVESTIGATIVE REPORTING (1976) (published by Indiana University Press).
4. *Id.* at 112–15.

The Art of Public Relations for Lawyers

6

Jill Lewis

TODAY, AMERICANS GET MOST of their information from print and broadcast media. From coast to coast and around the world, 24 hours a day, the public learns, laughs, cries, understands, and forms opinions due to news. Breaking news, feature stories, announcements, and commentary flash electronically across television and computer screens, appear boldly in newspaper and magazine headlines, and project repeatedly from AM and FM radio stations. Journalists seek people, visuals, and data to fill the coveted air time and print space; what and who gets on, or in, influences the way millions of people think and behave.

Savvy lawyers understand the power of this competitive environment and are learning how to use media visibility as a strategy to win business and develop their practices. Exposure to key audiences drives sales, promotes causes and industries, and draws attention to businesses, issues, products, services—*and people*. Lawyers and law firms are seizing the opportunity to create positive perceptions about their services through media visibility. Visibility—as it refers to image, identity, and presence—affects the business of practicing law.

Moreover, with downsizing a national trend and competition a daily challenge, lawyers today realize the need to focus on bottom-line issues such as practice development, client retention, and recruiting and keeping outstanding professional and support staff—in addition to counseling clients and winning cases.

Public Relations: What It Is, and How It Can Help

Effective public relations can enhance a firm's reputation. You build your firm's image and reputation every day. You are a walking, talking spokesperson for yourself, your firm, and your profession. According to Steve Frankel, senior vice president and director of corporate public affairs for GCI in Atlanta, "In matters of public relations, lawyers traditionally have counseled silence. But times are changing and while openness with the media is still a contentious subject among members of the bar, many influential lawyers have recognized the strategic advantage of public relations."[1]

Public relations is the subtle management of public perception, which over time leads "buyers" to believe in the quality of your service and the rightness of using that service. The wise, ethical, and fair-minded use of media relations can increase your business's goodwill with key audiences. It communicates to your audiences (1) who you are, (2) that you practice in an area that could meet their needs, (3) where and how your business operates, and (4) that you could be the right choice for representation.

Public relations and advertising are often confused. With advertising, you *pay* for a message by purchasing space with an electronic or print outlet for a specific audience. Advertising is useful, but it can produce residual negative effects, such as instilling distrust, appearing too self- serving, or being prone to exaggeration. Public relations, on the other hand, is *free* exposure; it positions a message through electronic or print media to help you gain positive visibility with your audiences. Though you do not have control over the end result of media coverage, you generally get the perceptual benefits resulting from unbiased, credible reporting.

Someone who is visible in respected media—quoted repeatedly as an authority on an issue or event—gains a reputation of respectability and credibility. Reporters seek out leading authorities and knowledgeable, respected experts for background and commentary. You can be among them.

The Truth about Reporters

Dealing with reporters often is like the practice of law; it can be an adversarial business. But usually reporters who seem to act like the opposition are following an ethical and professional journalistic code.

As discussed more thoroughly in other chapters, remembering certain things about journalists contributes to smooth interactions. For example, practicing the Golden Rule helps. So does noting that reporters are in the business of being the first ones to disseminate the facts, expose the story, or get the exclusive. That's what sells papers, interests viewers, and captures listeners. And although journalists tend to emphasize conflict and dissension, they seek the news value of every story, considering how it affects their specific audiences. On the front page, journalists write in anticipation of readers who ask, "What's happening in the world today that I should know as a citizen of my community, nation, and world?" On the business page, journalists presume readers who ask, "What is happening in the world today that I should know as an investor to protect or advance my financial interests?" Because of ever-present time constraints, reporters must eventually go with a story, with or without your comment. Finally, remember that the media strive to present all points of view in an unbiased manner, and inaccuracies often are the results of inadequate information— the refusal of an important source to furnish relevant facts or opinion, or insufficient time to gather such information.

Press Kits and News Releases

Print materials are important proactive tools that can be used to develop visibility. You may want to hire a public relations professional to draft your news releases and press kits. Professional communicators know how to craft materials that can be understood by a wide range of audiences, including reporters, and how to get them to the most appropriate journalists. In any event, whether you hire outside public relations counsel or delegate the responsibility to in-house staff, you should be aware of the following basics.

Press Kits: What They Include and How They Are Used

You can actively seek opportunities—placements in electronic and print media—through materials that plead your case in a professional, distinguished manner. Press kits are packages (usually presented in pocket portfolios) that present background information about you and your firm. A well-written press package should introduce you to reporters and provide information they can use in their stories; it should also be convenient to maintain on file. A press kit may include these items:

- Background information about you: your resumé, and a brief biography that indicates your areas of specialty, important cases, current and previous positions, memberships and affiliations, published articles and speaking engagements, and education
- Firm brochure or brief history: description of partners and staff, areas of specialty, key cases, and mission statement
- Black-and-white, reproducible photographs
- Pertinent news releases
- Copies of articles in which you or your firm have been mentioned (known as "clips")

News Releases: What They Should Achieve

News releases are excellent tools for bringing attention to businesses, events, persons, decisions, and other newsworthy items. Following the basic "who/what/when/where/why" format, news releases should tell the important facts first, capture the reader's interest, and include your name and phone number so the reporter can contact you. (See Chapter 7 for more in-depth discussions about press releases.) A warning: Use news releases judiciously—too many will fall on deaf ears. Consider these tips by Tony Mauro, legal reporter for *USA Today:*[2]

1. Don't waste time—yours or the reporter's. (*USA Today* is a national publication, and does not print law firm news such as announcements of new partners or openings of new offices.)
2. Minimize follow-up phone calls. Call once, only to confirm receipt of the release and to invite the reporter to call you with any questions.
3. Be timely. Moving fast means calling the reporter as soon as you hear about a ruling or verdict (if it happened yesterday, it is usually too late). If you have said you are available as an expert, then be informed about the materials and be ready to talk when the reporter calls.
4. Know the reporter (including the correct spelling of his or her name and the beat he or she covers) and what the publication usually prints.
5. Hire a public relations firm, at least for major projects that require some in-depth knowledge of how the news media work.
6. If you have in-house staff do the job, give it high priority and assign it to a lawyer or administrator who has written for newspapers or has had some training in public relations.
7. A well-timed, short, and targeted press release or telephone call that tells a reporter something that helps him or her do the job or look smart is always welcome.

Litigation Journalism

According to Carole E. Gorney, associate professor of journalism at Lehigh University, "Litigation journalism, the planned use and/or manipulation of the news and information media to promote the positions of plaintiffs and attorneys involved in civil lawsuits, refers both to the efforts used by those attempting to influence the public opinion through the news media, and to the media coverage itself. Organizations that are easy targets of often baseless litigation must learn and use the techniques of litigation public relations or risk losing the battle (and maybe the war) before firing their first legal shot in defense."3

Examples of litigation journalism are most numerous in product liability cases, but they also can be found in cases involving allegations of malpractice, personal injury, race or gender discrimination, and sexual harassment. Litigation journalism has become part of many lawyers' case strategies, and can provide positive exposure for the lawyers in the process; when you are quoted, the attention is as much on you—the legal expert on the issue—as it is on the issue itself. However, Gorney warns that litigation journalism can be abused, and many persons and entities—including Congress and the courts—are beginning to lose patience with certain litigation practices.

When the Reporter Calls

Congratulations! You have received a call from a reporter. How you respond from now on can mean the difference between success and failure—positive or negative visibility, or no visibility at all. Before making your decision about granting an interview or providing information, first tell the reporter you need some background details. Ask questions such as these:

- ♦ What is the basis for the call? Possibilities could include the following:

    1. The reporter needs a source; you could be it.
    2. The reporter got your press release and may want to do a story.
    3. The reporter is returning your call.

- ♦ Is the reporter writing for print, radio, television or computer? When will the interview be broadcast or printed? If a broadcast interview, will it be live or taped?
- ♦ What is the reporter's time frame? That is, by what time/day does he or she need the information? (Always try to return the reporter's call immediately, if only to determine the reporter's deadline.)

♦ What is the subject of the story, and the reporter's angle in reporting it?

♦ What is the reporter's knowledge of the subject? Is the reporter a lawyer as well? Does the reporter usually cover legal issues? Does he or she generally understand legislative issues and the details of a case? Is the reporter local, or from another area of the country?

♦ What is the reporter's motivation for doing the story? You can ask, "What led you to do this story? What interests you most about this topic?"

♦ Who are the audiences? Are they local, national, or international? Is the story to be read by the public at large? Other lawyers? Law students? Professionals in a given subject area? What are the demographics—women, men, or both? What are the readers' ages, incomes, and education levels?

♦ What does the reporter want from you? Is he or she working on a breaking news story, or a feature piece such as a profile? Is he or she talking to many sources, or will you be the main source? Is the reporter looking for someone who is on one side of the issues? Does the reporter need a source with detailed knowledge of a case, or more general knowledge of the area? Is general background needed, or will you be quoted in the finished piece? In what context will the report appear? Will it be part of a larger story? What is the reporter's perspective?

Deciding Whether to Grant the Interview

Grant an interview if it is to your advantage or benefit to do so, or to your disadvantage not to do so. Remember that the story will be written with or without you. Generally, you should talk with the media if it would benefit you to get your side of a negative or difficult story out to the public. If you do not provide the information, the reporter probably will turn to someone else. If the reporter talks with a source from your firm, you have a chance to shape ("spin") the story and have your viewpoint included.

Generally, if you believe it would be best not to talk with the reporter, then you should say so instead of simply stating, "No comment." You could offer reasons such as the following:

- "We prefer to put forth our position with supportive evidence at the appropriate time."
- "We do not want to add to any misconceptions about this case."
- "We do not want to contribute to any possibility that this case might be tried in the media before trial begins; you'll hear our case in the courtroom."

Even if you cannot talk about the topic this time, you can turn the call into an opportunity by encouraging the reporter to call you again when he or she needs information or a source. Keep the reporter's name and telephone number in your file so you can approach him or her when you do have a story or a comment.

According to Debra Coudert Sweeney, public relations director of Cramer-Krassell in Orlando, Florida, "One medium that should be scrupulously avoided is tabloid television."[4] She gives the following advice:[5]

- Do not participate; send a written response to any inquiry from a television tabloid setting forth your position, backed with facts.
- Instead of spending time preparing for this kind of interview, use publicity and reprints of publicity to disseminate positive words about your organization.
- Approach a credible print news source and offer a counter-interview to achieve balance.
- Be alert, because tabloids often do not play fair.

Tabloid television has an enormous following because of its often sensational content, and the astute lawyer needs to evaluate the opportunity for exposure on a case-by-case basis.

Preparation: A Strategy for Success

Assuming you decide to talk further with the media, you should spend some time preparing your for your interview. According to

Chris Barnett in *Public Relations Executive Report,* 90 percent of success depends on preparation.[6] You would not try a case without a strategy; you should not give an interview without one either.

Before the Interview

Begin by doing the following:

1. Do research on the reporter and/or the story. Promise to get back to the reporter within a specified time (before deadline). Tell the reporter that you need a few hours (or a few days if time permits) to familiarize yourself with the facts of the case or to consult with a colleague.
2. Develop your message. Know what you want to accomplish in the interview before the interview begins. Write a mission statement—one concise sentence that describes your view. This statement can be repeated several times during the interview to underscore your point and make it memorable. Add interest and credibility with examples, stories, analogies, numbers, or a third-party endorsement such as, "According to the American Bar Association . . ."

During the Interview

Next, keep in mind the following "dos and don'ts"—they will help you articulate well-conceived, image-enhancing responses to the interviewer's questions. Remember that different reporters have different definitions of "off the record"—if you do not want something to appear in print, don't say it. And do not let your guard down; the interview is not over until the reporter leaves or hangs up the telephone.

Dos and Don'ts

The "dos":

1. Speak in conversational, understandable terms appropriate for the audience.
2. Be succinct—speak in sound bites (meaningful, colorful, quotable phrases).

3. Respond to questions with conclusions first (the head-line), and then give facts, examples, anecdotes, statistics, pertinent personal experiences, and reasons.
4. Know where you are going with a point.
5. Write two or three questions you want the reporter to ask you. Then say, "These are the toughest questions we've received on this case."
6. Personalize and humanize the message with anecdotes and examples.
7. Emphasize the points you want the reporter to write by saying, "This is what it's all about."
8. Tell the truth.
9. If you need to do further research to respond appropriately, promise to get the information and call the reporter back within a specified deadline.

The "don'ts":

1. Don't answer third-party quotes you haven't heard.
2. Don't repeat negative or offensive questions.
3. Don't criticize peers.
4. Don't lose your temper or argue.
5. If at all possible, don't say, "No comment." Instead, explain why you cannot answer (client confidentiality or pending litigation, for example). Otherwise you may seem guilty, evasive, and/or uncooperative.
6. Don't use legal jargon.
7. Don't wander.
8. Don't evade or guess at an answer.

Control the Flow

You may not be the one who is asking the questions, but you can be in control of the interview. Here's how to make sure the right questions get asked, so you get your message across.

1. Keep your mission statement on top of your mind, and find every opportunity to repeat it.
2. Zero in on the heart of the issue.

3. Bridge (move the conversation) from answering the reporter's questions to the points you want to make—your message. Bridge phrases could be these:

- ◆ "What this really means is . . ."
- ◆ "But the important point is . . ."
- ◆ "Yes, but keep in mind that . . ."

Body Talk

The way you look and sound is very important. Experts say that we get our first impression of someone in the 10 or 20 seconds that pass after meeting. This is especially important for broadcast media, when audiences hear and see you for themselves without the interpretation of the reporter. Practice in front of a mirror. Role play with a friend, colleague, or spouse. Videotape yourself if you have time, and invite the critique of a professional media trainer. Here are some body language tips:

1. Look into the reporter's eyes and don't look away. Don't look at the camera or shift your eyes.
2. Unbutton your suit jacket when seated and tuck the rear hem of a skirt under you.
3. Don't slouch, sway, or wear clashing colors.
4. Smile (unless you are talking about a tragic event), make eye contact, and relax and make gestures to give your voice some power and to make you look natural on camera.
5. Lean forward when you are talking, and keep your arms and hands open to show you are accepting and not on the defensive.
6. Don't touch your ears (a sign of deception), keep your hands away from your face (indicates you want to hide), and don't put your hands on the back of your neck (shows fear).

The Follow-Up Phase

Your opportunities for visibility do not stop when the interview ends. The story has yet to be written and appear before your audiences. Tomorrow is another day, with another story to be written, and another source to be interviewed. You have begun to build a relationship with the reporter; now is the time to nurture it.

Reporters can seem temperamental or annoyed if approached incorrectly. To make the most of your relationship, consider the following suggestions (some of which are discussed in other chapters). First, do not ask to review a story before it appears. Instead, offer to be available if the reporter has further questions or needs to check details for accuracy. Second, fulfill your promises; in particular, send information within the time promised so that it will be useful to the reporter. And third, do not complain about a reporter to an editor or to the reporter's colleagues.

After the story appears, you could do the following:

♦ Call the reporter if you believe you have been misquoted or treated unfairly. Calmly explain what you see as the error, or write a letter to that effect.

♦ Offer to provide additional assistance.

♦ Get clips—copies of the article in which you are quoted or mentioned. You may need to hire a clipping service (a service that employs trained readers to find articles that mention you in local and national publications). Using these articles enhances your credibility as an authority; they also provide excellent inserts for press kits, handouts at seminars, and marketing materials.

♦ Call the reporter when you have a story that you think will interest him or her. But be cautious that you don't overdo it. If you overuse the reporter's telephone number or e-mail address, you may be suspected of having ulterior motives and distrusted as a spokesperson. Inappropriate calls, too many calls, and wandering messages affect your credibility.

♦ Never give out a reporter's telephone number without his or her permission. Although the telephone is a reporter's lifeline, it often is misused by errant publicity seekers.

Be patient. Media relations is a building process that gets results over time. It takes time to build relationships with reporters, and time to realize the positive impact of a number of meaningful placements (quotes and/or mentions in the press). As reported in *Lawyers' Weekly USA,* Seattle public relations counselor Dean Katz explains that public relations "is the steady drumbeat of *another* verdict, *another* settlement, *another* quote on a topical issue on TV."[7]

Using communications techniques to enhance the visibility of your firm is a means to an end. It is a process that starts with a certain mind-set—that positive messages communicated to your audiences on a regular basis can yield high returns for your practice.

Summary: The Quick-Review Checklists

It's time you explored the value of public relations for your firm. Communicating with the media can be one of the most efficient ways to develop interest in your business. You may be a solo practitioner, a member of a mid- to large-size firm, or in-house counsel. You are the expert in what you do, and a potential source for journalists—locally as well as nationally. The next time a reporter calls, you can be ready. Get out these quick-review checklists—they summarize the issues discussed in this chapter—and capitalize on the media opportunity.

Top 10 Tips for Dealing with Reporters

1. Prepare your message before the interview.
2. Establish ground rules before the interview.
3. Don't speak in legalese.
4. Stick to the subject.
5. Keep your promises within the reporter's deadline.
6. Return calls promptly.
7. Be on time for interviews.
8. Use confident, direct body language.
9. Stay in control by bridging to your message.
10. Use considerate telephone etiquette.

When-the-Reporter-Calls Checklist

❏ What is the basis for the call?
❏ Is the reporter writing for print, radio, television, or computer?
❏ What is the reporter's time frame?
❏ What is the subject of the story and the reporter's angle?
❏ What is the reporter's knowledge of the subject?
❏ Who are the audiences?
❏ What does the reporter want from you?

Preparation Checklist

❏ Do your research on the reporter and/or the story.
❏ Develop your message.

Interview Checklist (You're On!)

The "Dos"

❏ Speak in conversational, understandable terms appropriate to the audience.
❏ Be succinct.
❏ Give the headline first; then back it up.
❏ Know where you are going with a point.
❏ Write two or three questions you want the reporter to ask you.
❏ Personalize and humanize the message.
❏ Emphasize the points you want the reporter to write.
❏ Tell the truth.
❏ Promise to get back to the reporter with additional information if needed.

The "Don'ts"

❏ Don't answer third-party quotes you haven't heard.
❏ Don't repeat negative or offensive questions.
❏ Don't criticize peers.
❏ Don't lose your temper or argue.
❏ Don't say, "No comment," if at all possible.
❏ Don't evade or guess at an answer.

Be in Control

- ❑ Keep your mission statement at the top of your mind.
- ❑ Zero in on the heart of the issue.
- ❑ Bridge from answering the reporter's questions to the points you want to make.

Endnotes

1. *In Defense of Lawyers,* THE PUBLIC RELATIONS STRATEGIST (Winter 1995).

2. *Pitching Reporters on Law Firm News,* LEGAL TIMES, June 5, 1995.

3. *The New Rules of Litigation Public Relations,* THE PUBLIC RELATIONS STRATEGIST (Spring 1995).

4. *Not Dealing with Tabloid Television,* THE PUBLIC RELATIONS STRATEGIST (Summer 1995).

5. *Id.*

6. *Learning to Talk to the Media,* VIS A VIS (August 1992).

7. *An Alternative to Advertising: Using Public Relations to Build Your Practice,* LAWYERS WEEKLY USA (Feb. 27, 1995).

Writing Press Releases

Jill Lewis

7

WRITING NEWS RELEASES draws on skills you have already honed in legal writing—organizing information logically, communicating clearly, and getting to the point. What differs is the audience—a reporter or editor on deadline who is skimming quickly to find story ideas. You must keep the reporter's or editor's needs uppermost in mind. You can do this by following these steps:

1. Find the right kind of story.
2. Find the right publication and target the story to a specific editor.
3. Ascertain the facts and verify all information.
4. Write in the appropriate format.
5. If the story is an important one, follow up with a call.

What Is Newsworthy?

Law firms issue two types of releases: those raising law firm visibility and those providing information about client transactions.

The Law Firm

The election of new partners or managing partners, lateral hires, appointments, and awards are all occasions for press releases (though the extent to which media consider these items newsworthy varies). The same applies to pro bono activities, office relocations, speeches, and publications. Law firm merger stories have particular appeal, because the process of transacting a merger typically interests a reporter as much as the fact that the merger was accomplished. You can intrigue the reporter to do further investigation by noting briefly why the firms merged, their collective strengths, and how the situation came about.

To achieve maximum benefit from your press releases, you should target them to places that regularly collect these announcements, rather than "shotgunning" them for general distribution.

Client Transactions

Releases involving a client need to be evaluated not simply for their newsworthiness, but also for the degree to which they benefit and affect the client. Announcements ordinarily concern a lawsuit being filed or resolved. The story may focus on a verdict won, a case dismissed, or a particularly noteworthy settlement or award. A note of caution: Even if the information that you write is available in public records, you must have your client's consent—not necessarily for the wording of the release, but certainly for its dissemination. Beyond that, attempts to "spin" litigation or mold public opinion usually call for consultation with a public relations professional. He or she can advise you on the best ways of conveying your message.

Creating a Mailing List

You should prepare a mailing list in advance so you can issue press releases quickly. The list should be separated into categories, such as those listed below, so you can target mailings:

♦ Business publications or business reporters at general newspapers and magazines
♦ Legal publications (both daily and monthly; also local and national), including state and local bar association newsletters and journals
♦ Electronic outlets (television, online publications, and radio)
♦ Wire services such as Associated Press, Reuters, and the Businesswire
♦ Alumni publications
♦ Local daily and weekly newspapers and magazines

If at all possible, avoid sending your releases to titles (such as, "Attention: Business Editor"). Take the time to learn who on the masthead would have interest in your story. Of course, this obliges you to update your mailing list periodically, as people are reassigned or move.

For lists of legal publications, contact the reference librarian at your local law library. Also, the librarian at your public library can point you to media directories that list addresses and fax numbers of national news outlets.

Tone and Style

Make Your Writing Simple and Clear

Although the recipients of your releases are journalists, the ultimate consumers are usually nonlawyers (unless the news is targeted to legal publications). You should strive to avoid using legal jargon when writing for laypeople. If you cannot, then explain or define terms immediately after their appearance in the article. The more obtuse your language, the harder the reporter must work at paraphrasing it for a mass audience. Errors can often creep into a piece during the translation process. Ideally, your phrasing should be so simple and apt that the reporter can quote it directly or appropriate it altogether—a standard journalistic practice.

Avoid the Committee Approach

A word of caution: Some law firms require a number of partners and even committees to review press releases before their dissemination. Sometimes, egos creep into the editing process—inflating an accomplishment or qualifying a statement until it is practically meaningless. Use your skills as an advocate to explain that the release is being written for journalists. Few things grate on a reporter more than releases that are obviously self-serving or filled with legalese.

The Plan of Attack

Let's assume you have decided a press release is in order and have targeted the appropriate publications. What's next?

Collect and Check Your Information

To reiterate a recurring theme: Time is of the essence in the news game—reporters do not want to spend it needlessly. You can help by checking to make sure names, titles, dates, and facts are accurate. Do not guess, do not exaggerate, and above all else, do not lie. Just as you would advise a client in a deposition, "If you don't know the answer, don't speculate."

State the Most Important News First

Your first sentence is the "lead" that answers the questions of who, what, when, where, why, and how. The convention is to write in the third person and pack all this information in a single sentence. If the sentence gets unwieldy, however, break it in two. The one-sentence rule applies only to the first paragraph. All subsequent paragraphs should be brief. Use active voice whenever possible. And remember that most newspapers are geared to someone with a high-school education.

Keep It Short

Your release should never run more than three pages. Use the inverted-pyramid style of ordering paragraphs by decreasing importance. Whenever you state a name, identify the person clearly ("Jane Jones, who coordinated the defense . . ."). But keep the identification brief so the reader does not become bogged down. A graceful way of listing someone's credentials is to add a detail with each subsequent reference ("Fred Johnson, Chair of the Litigation Department, negotiated the settlement. Johnson, a graduate of Harvard Law School, . . ."). Lengthy identifications, such as a description of a corporation's holdings and activities, belong at the end of the story.

Follow AP Style

Just as *The Bluebook: A Uniform System of Citation* governs style in legal writing, *The Associated Press Stylebook and Libel Manual* states the conventions for newswriting. Refer to it for abbreviations of states, identification of courts, and handling of numerals. Following AP style lends credibility to your release.

Keep It Simple

In newswriting, a turn-of-phrase matters less than clarity and simplicity. Make sure your story flows smoothly. Break down complicated matters item by item, with bullets.

The Style Checklist

Using the following checklist will help you organize your press releases for distribution.

- ❑ Input your name, or that of another individual at your office, as the contact person who can talk to reporters.
- ❑ Compose the headline, centered in all caps, and double-spaced, like this:

JOHN DOE JOINS THE ATLANTA OFFICE

OF XYZ LAW FIRM.

❏ First paragraph: Get to the point quickly. The main information ("news nugget") should be at the top, with supporting facts at the bottom.

❏ For persons mentioned, give a full name, hometown, and full title of position. (Note: Use the full name in the first mention; last name only in subsequent mentions. Do not use courtesy titles such as Mr., Mrs., Ms., or Miss.)

❏ Following paragraph(s): Present other pertinent involvement, such as community, board, or charity participation.

❏ Following paragraph(s): Present education.

❏ Closing paragraph: Include firm boilerplate information, such as this:

XY&Z, Ltd., is a leading Atlanta-based law firm specializing in products liability litigation. With offices in Chicago, New York, and San Francisco, the firm provides legal counsel to Fortune 500 corporations and other businesses across the country.

❏ If your release is more than one page, insert "—more—" centered at the bottom of the first page.

❏ Indicate the end of the release with the symbols "###" centered on the page.

Examples of Press Releases

Example 1: Announcement of Important Verdict or Judicial Decision

FOR IMMEDIATE RELEASE   Contact: [NAME]

Date: [PHONE NUMBER]

[NAME OF FIRM] WINS $200 MILLION VERDICT

FOR XYZ CORPORATION

[CITY, STATE] - [NAME OF FIRM] announced today that the [NAME OF CITY]-based law firm, a national leader in admiralty and maritime litigation, was successful in obtaining a jury verdict that awarded $200 million in punitive damages to its client, XYZ Corporation. In [NAME OF CASE], tried in the [NAME OF COURT], the decision was noteworthy in that . . .

"[QUOTE]," says [NAME OF LEAD COUNSEL].

[NAME OF DEFENDANT] is expected to appeal.

[LAW FIRM BOILERPLATE]

###

Example 2: Personnel Announcement

FOR IMMEDIATE RELEASE   Contact: [NAME]

Date: [PHONE NUMBER]

[NAME OF HOMETOWN] RESIDENT [NAME OF NEW PARTNER]

JOINS [NAME OF FIRM]

[CITY, STATE] - [NAME OF NEW PARTNER] of [HOMETOWN], has joined [LAW FIRM], [CITY]'s leading criminal defense firm, to head the firm's securities department. [SURNAME OF NEW PARTNER] will assist with practice development as well as securities litigation for clients such as [NAMES].

"[QUOTE]," says [NAME OF FIRM MANAGING PARTNER].

[SURNAME OF NEW PARTNER] formerly was partner at [NAME OF PRIOR FIRM], where he represented clients such as [NAMES].

[SURNAME OF NEW PARTNER] is [LIST AFFILIATIONS AND AWARDS].

[SURNAME OF NEW PARTNER] lives in [LOCAL NEIGHBOR-HOOD] where he [AFFILIATIONS].

He holds a law degree from [NAME OF LAW SCHOOL] and a bachelor's degree in [DEGREE] from [NAME OF UNDERGRADUATE SCHOOL].

[FIRM BOILERPLATE]

###

Media Interviews: How to Appear Confident and in Control

8

Spring Asher and Marilyn Ringo

BASED ON THE RESEARCH of social scientist Dr. Albert Mehrabian,[1] 55 – 38 – 7 is the critical statistic for understanding how people evaluate you as a communicator: 55 percent of the impression you make is your presence, 38 percent is your voice energy, and only 7 percent is the content of your remarks. This statistic means that no matter how valid your information, the "93 percent" factors determine whether the listener will stay tuned to what you say.

Your presentation skills are important in dealing with all media. With print media, your presence and the conviction in your voice "sell" the reporter who is the conduit for your story. With radio, your voice sells the story. With television, you personify the message. People typically have strengths in different areas. For example, in the polls following the Kennedy/Nixon presidential debates, Nixon won on radio, while Kennedy won on television.

Physical Presentation:
The 93-Percent Solution

Kent Alexander, a partner at the Atlanta firm of King & Spalding, was frequently interviewed by and under fire from the media as the U.S. Attorney during the bombings at Centennial Olympic Park, abortion clinics, and the Otherside Lounge in Atlanta. Although he was confident about his information, he said that he "learned from experience that presentation is part of the message."[2]

Alexander has several suggestions.[3] Before the cameras roll, straighten your tie if you do not want to appear harried. Be aware of the expression on your face, even when you are not speaking— a camera person may take cutaway shots to insert in the story. When talking to reporters, turn your whole face to them. A sideways glance at them and others will make you look shifty-eyed. In a seated interview, sit upright. (Alexander also pulls his jacket down and sits on his coattails.) Why should you bother with all these tips? Because first impressions count. Your partners care, your parents care, and, as the well-known Washington reporter Helen Thomas says, colleagues never seem to notice the pithy question she asks, instead they usually comment on her hair!

You can enhance your performance in an interview by addressing your posture, gestures, eye contact, voice energy, dress style, and nervousness.

Use Good Posture

A confident posture adds credibility to interviews. You should sit up, with your body bent slightly forward to show interest and a readiness to share information. Hands and arms should be open, not crossed or clasped. People who lean or sit back in a chair look bored or defensive. Watch Sam Donaldson and Cokie Roberts on ABC's *Sunday Morning*. The way they sit at the round table is a good example of seated presence. When standing, you should lead from the chest and stand on the balls of your feet, not back on your heels.

Control Your Gestures

You should take care not to use motions (such as playing with your glasses or using overly dramatic gestures) that distract from your message. However, an occasional firm gesture, when consistent with your speech, can add energy to your message.

Keep Eye Contact

If you lock your eyes on the host or reporter, you are less likely to appear shifty, nervous, or insincere. It is not necessary to look at the television camera. It will find you.

Use Your Face

You can add energy and conviction to your interview by using your facial features. Use your eyebrows to communicate an emotion. Soften and relax your face. Lift your cheeks. Speak and listen with a warm face. A smile is a great disarmer. If people like you, they tend to trust you and believe your message.

Enhance Your Voice Energy

In radio and television interviews, voice variety projects conviction. Listeners can hear a smile or a frown in your voice. Your conviction needs to come across. "Punch up" the important words. Television anchors underline a word on the TelePrompTer to add emphasis. They pause before an important point and as they change thoughts. Vocal variety (louder, softer, faster, slower) reinforces your conviction and keeps the interview lively. Print reporters also need to hear an energetic interview, so they can transfer your enthusiasm and sincerity to readers.

Dress to Enhance Your Credibility

Clothing, jewelry, and makeup should never be used in a way that detracts from your message or your credibility. For women: Solid colors look best on television. A dark suit and your most becoming colored blouse work best. If you wear a dress, remember that a jacket will add presence. Limit the amount of jewelry you wear, and avoid clanky necklaces and bracelets. For men: A blue or gray suit with a light-colored shirt, such as off-white, is good for television. A red tie gives you a sense of energy. A jacket, even without a tie, adds to your presence.

For television interviews, you should not wear white clothing if you have dark skin, and you should not wear black clothing if you have light skin. The high contrast forces the camera to compensate, and the result is unflattering.

Makeup for television is also important. Women should wear additional blush and powder to avoid a pale, anemic look. Men can use a tanning gel to achieve a healthy look, especially in winter.

Controlling Nervousness

Being nervous is normal. Expect to be nervous. Fifty percent of controlling nervousness is knowing your information. You can also help yourself by breathing from your abdomen. Shallow breathing from the chest makes you less relaxed and results in a higher voice. Moreover, with an open presence, solid eye contact, and a relaxed facial expression, you will look confident, even when you don't feel that way.

Mental Preparation: The 7-Percent Salvation

Henry Kissinger, former U.S. Secretary of State, said to reporters, "Does anyone have any questions for the answers I have prepared?" You too should always prepare for questions you think could be asked. Never assume that you are at the mercy of the interviewer. Take control. Know the points you want to make. Collect illustrations (sound bites) that bring each of your points to life. Only knowledge gives you the confidence to look and sound in control.

If the interview is to be done in your office, establish ground rules in advance. Learn about the topic and what the interviewer wants to know. If you have a time deadline, state it in advance. By taking a moment with the reporter up front, you can establish rapport, determine the extent of the reporter's knowledge, and possibly work together to get a better story.

"Bundling"—Keeping Your Message Focused

"Bundle" your message objective and two or three points (A, B, and C) into one answer. Give the answer bundle early in the interview. State that these are the subjects you are prepared to discuss. Setting the agenda protects you from questions that are off the subject. Then, when you answer each question, reinforce one of your three points and illustrate a sound bite with a story, statistic, or analogy. Here is an example:

Question: How do you feel about current bank regulations?

Answer: They have three functions: (A) they protect consumers, (B) they protect customers, and (C) they protect the community. Let me give you an example.

Taking Control in a Press Conference

To take control in a press conference, you should decide the location, establish the type and number of questions you will answer, and determine—in advance—exactly what information you will disclose. You can also help control the tenor of the press conference by "bridging" to the message you most want to communicate.

Turn Negatives into Positives: An Example of "Bridging"

Lawyer Darryl Cohen, of Greenberg Traurig in Atlanta, was defending a client in a high-profile arson case. He received no fewer than 100 calls a day from the national, international, and local media. Rather than avoiding them, he took control and used the media to his advantage by calling press conferences at his offices.

First, he controlled the venue. "It was my ball game. I had them in my court."[4] Second, he controlled the questioning. When questions were being hurled at him left and right, he told the reporters, "I can take only one question at a time. Let me start with the reporter in the back."[5] In an opening statement, he limited the amount of time and number of questions he would take. And third, he controlled the information being disseminated over the airwaves. "It's kind of like playing football. You're going for a long pass and you want them to think you're going to run. I turned my client from a defendant into a victim by hanging photos of her bruised and battered face on the wall behind me. I was able to move the reporters from questions about her problems with alcohol to her boyfriend's abusive treatment. I gave them access to my client and also gave them stuff they didn't know they wanted."[6] When questions about her alcohol problem arose ("Isn't it true she's an alcoholic?"), Cohen remembers he answered the question briefly, "I can't say," and then "bridged" to his information—"I can tell you this poor kid has been abused."[7] The case turned in his favor. Cohen's client paid a fine and spent some time in a halfway house. Today she's again enjoying a high-profile, successful career.

Taking Control in an Interview

Never Reinforce a Negative

You should always state an answer in positive terms. The wisdom of this advice becomes evident in the following two examples. When President Ronald Reagan was asked about the proposed Equal Rights Amendment, he originally gave a negative answer. Later he said, "I am in favor of equal rights for women, but I feel that there are alternative ways to achieve this goal." He then went on to explain his point. In a famous speech, President Richard Nixon stated, "I am not a crook." He should have said, "I am an honest man."

Show Caring

Bill Cannon, of Cannon, Meyer Vonn Bremen & Gross, LLP, in Albany, Georgia, represented WALB-TV, the NBC affiliate in Albany, in seeking to have cameras in the courtroom during a murder trial in a nearby county. The district attorney and the defense lawyer opposed cameras in the courtroom. Some of the press coverage gave play to the victim's family members, who were on camera saying such things as, "I can't believe you're putting us through this. You're trying to be voyeurs during a horrible time." Cannon says his approach was to avoid being defensive and show that his clients cared. His response was, "We have great sympathy for the victims and we understand this is going to be a very difficult time for them. On the other hand, the very justice system they are relying on to bring justice to the accused also depends upon openness and it would teach a great civics lesson."[8] Cannon says he is always aware of his audience when doing interviews or press conferences, and in many cases, the audiences are the very judges trying his current and future cases.

Speak in Simple and Jargon-Free Language

"Gerry Spence, Roy Black, Roger Cossack, and Greta Van Susteren are all lawyers who are media stars," says Gail Evans, executive vice president of CNN.[9] "Most litigators are media friendly, because they are used to performing in front of a group. The problem occurs when they speak the language of a law school. The result is that they distance themselves from the average listener."[10] When interviewed, many lawyers make the mistake of performing for their colleagues. However, chances are that the audience contains more potential clients than colleagues. What makes a lawyer impressive to the media is an ability to do the following:

♦ Demystify the information
♦ Use simple language
♦ Speak in short, declarative sentences

Lawyers who succeed with the media have passion for their causes, and tell their stories so that anyone can understand them. Consequently, people believe them.

Prepare for the Ambush Interview

Lawyers can learn something from professional athletes and coaches who deliver effective messages to the media—they prepare for impromptu questions, and mentally shape their ideas as they leave the playing field. Before you meet the media or leave a courtroom, you should similarly prepare a statement and three points you will address. Reach into your mental reserves for analogies, statistics, and other bits of evidence that will bring your points to life.

Kevin Getzendanner of Arnall Golden & Gregory, LLP, in Atlanta, Georgia, was litigating a case in Charleston, South Carolina, concerning the possible construction of a hospital. The media were covering the case because there was considerable community resistance to the construction. Television cameras and reporters waited outside the courthouse each day. As much as Getzendanner and his team wanted to avoid the press, it was not possible. Getzendanner says, "We weren't in a position to let the other side advertise."[11]

Together with the public relations department of the hospital, he prepared for the inevitable on-camera appearances on the courthouse steps. "First of all, you have to remember that it is the client speaking," says Getzendanner, "[s]o you better know what they want to say and whether they want to say anything. We prepared talking points for ourselves and the client and honed a message to convert our litigation message into [television]-consumable form."[12] That is a short, pithy statement. Controlling the message in front of those cameras was a real win for Getzendanner and his client. The hospital construction was approved. As is true for most lawyers, Getzendanner says, "I like to be in control. When I faced those cameras I didn't feel defenseless. I was equipped."[13]

Press Conferences versus One-on-One Interviews

Kent Alexander's experience as U.S. Attorney offers insight into determining how to meet the media. A press conference is most efficient for "Big News." Planning ahead is key, and finding five quiet minutes to gather your thoughts immediately before the conference also helps. Reporters covering an interesting story appreciate your notifying them that you are available for the media, as they then believe they will get a special sound bite. When the story is important to you, but is something less than an earth-shattering event, offer an exclusive to a reporter and you may get coverage.

Consider the following factors to determine whether a one-on-one contact or a press conference is the most effective way to communicate your message.

- ◆ Advantages of a one-on-one interview:

  1. Offers more personal interaction than a press conference
  2. Targets specific media questions
  3. Establishes rapport with individual members of the media

- ◆ Disadvantages of a one-on-one interview:

  1. Takes more time than a press conference
  2. Does not address a large number of media inquiries as quickly as a press conference
  3. Offers less control over the "one message approach"

- ◆ Advantages of a press conference:

  1. Permits the speaker to control the time
  2. Allows news to get out more quickly to more media members
  3. Contains rumors more effectively
  4. Allows for advance knowledge of 85 percent of the questions, so the speaker can be prepared (President Bush's advisors achieved this accuracy.)

- ◆ Disadvantages of a press conference:

  1. Creates potential for difficulty in controlling a roomful of reporters clamoring for information
  2. Can result in a heated and volatile situation
  3. Provides an outlet for the tendency of reporters to become aggressive in a peer situation

Practice

Practicing the following techniques will help you come across with confidence and credibility in any type of media appearance.

❑ Do your homework before an interview.
Read an article by the print reporter. Listen to the interviewer's radio program. Watch the television host or reporter.

❑ Watch television without sound.
Study the gestures, body language, and energy of the speakers.

❑ Study your information.
You cannot give it away until you "own" it.

❑ Practice speaking on videotape.
Study your facial gestures (eyebrows, mouth, and eyes), your posture, and your voice quality.

❑ Practice "bridging" in daily conversation.

❑ Keep a file of "quotable quotes" and "gee whiz" facts.
Use examples in daily conversation.

❑ Have a mock interview session at the office.
Make a point and give an illustration. Play "Beat the Clock." Can you do it in 10 to 15 seconds?

❑ Listen to or watch interview sessions on the *Today Show, Good Morning America,* or *Larry King Live.*

❑ "Tape and ape."
Learn from the communications pros. Tape a favorite communicator, transcribe the interview, and then try mimicking the style, pacing, and voice variety until you develop your own.

❑ Practice bundling—group your main points.

❑ Practice on the telephone.
Know the points you want to make. Make your points and illustrate them. Summarize at the end of the conversation.

In sum, you need to prepare and practice. The 93-percent solution, plus the 7-percent salvation, will give you the skills you need to meet the media 100-percent ready.

Endnotes

1. Spring Asher & Wicke Chambers, Wooing and Winning Business (1997).
2. Interview with Kent Alexander.

3. *Id.*
4. Interview with Darryl Cohen.
5. *Id.*
6. *Id.*
7. *Id.*
8. Interview with William E. Cannon, Jr.
9. Interview with Gail Evans.
10. *Id.*
11. Interview with Kevin B. Getzendanner.
12. *Id.*
13. *Id.*

Litigation That Attracts the Media

9

Peter C. Canfield

MUCH HAS BEEN SAID, written, and even decided about the professional obligations governing lawyer comments to the media, but most of the discussion centers on the constitutionality and enforceability of state bar rules purportedly designed to protect the integrity and impartiality of the applicable tribunal.

For the lawyer in a position to seek or likely to face media attention, easily forgotten but at least as important is the lawyer's obligation to the client. The principle that should control any lawyer's interaction with the media about any case is that it is *not* the lawyer's case—it is the client's.

Assisting the Client

Conferring with the client in advance of any media contact—or, at the least, any substantive response—is essential. Even leaving aside potential attorney-client privilege issues, lawyers often fail to appreciate fully that for many clients (and for a variety of issues), the public's perception of an ongoing lawsuit may be almost as important—or more important—than the outcome in the courtroom. For this reason, just as the license to represent the client in the courtroom does not afford a lawyer, absent an understanding with the client, broad discretion to make significant litigation decisions without consultation, the "whethers" and "hows" of interaction with the media are matters upon which the lawyer and client must reach mutual understanding and agreement.

Clients—even those who do not live for the latest lawyer joke—do not necessarily consider lawyers innately adept at media relations. Clients do not generally assume (as do many lawyers) that because of personal temperament and training in public speaking, lawyers are uniquely capable of positively shaping public opinion. More often than not, lawyers—particularly given their image as hired guns (and often opportunistic and disloyal ones at that)—are not a first choice as client spokespersons.

Clients nevertheless should and do appreciate the considerable assistance that lawyers can provide in connection with media coverage of their cases. Because of the perspective that a lawyer can provide, even the most sophisticated client would be unwise to undertake responding to the media without the lawyer's direct involvement.

The Lawyer's Unique Perspective

Lawyers have special training, experience, and knowledge that give them a unique perspective for dealing with the media. This in turn means they have certain responsibilities as advocates for their clients during media interactions.

Explaining the Public Nature of Litigation

The lawyer is in the best position to ensure that the client fully appreciates not only the litigation process, but also its public context. Individuals and companies often assume that even after a case has been filed, their disputes are private ones. They believe the lawyers will ensure—or a simple motion to the court will require—that it remain such. Such an assumption, often reinforced by lawyer or organized bar statements that any contact with the press is somehow unprofessional, may lead a client to ignore the media or to neglect preparation of a meaningful response. But the assumption is wrong and the lawyer should ensure the client understands that from the outset.

It should come as no surprise to lawyers, but may surprise many clients, that virtually all stages of the litigation process in this country are required to be public. This includes trials, pretrial proceedings, and, to a great extent, discovery; what a client says in a deposition one day may be filed in court tomorrow and the subject of news stories and general public evaluation the day following. By educating a client from the outset on the openness of the process, a lawyer may and should encourage a client to prepare for the media attention that often follows.

Evaluating the Effect of Media Statements on Litigation

The lawyer, given his or her stewardship of a case, is also in the best position to evaluate the effect of the client's proposed media statements on the litigation. As a general matter, clients do not appreciate the extent to which comments outside the courtroom can affect—for better or worse—the proceedings within it. The lawyer can and should ensure that what is being said outside the courtroom is accurate and the same as what is said within.

A recent Georgia personal injury case illustrates the point. An automobile manufacturer, stung by a compensatory damage award in a truck design-defect case and presumably eager to stem the effect of the award on the price of its publicly-traded stock, reportedly issued an immediate press release defending the safety of the design. At the same time, the manufacturer's lawyer was in court in the case's punitive-damages phase, attempting to convince the jury that the company had gotten the message that the design was defective. The contrary press release found its way into the hands of the plaintiff's lawyer, who used it in his rebuttal to make an effective argument for substantial punitive damages.

Maintaining Lawyer-Client Communications

The lesson is that the lawyer, even if not the client spokesperson, needs to know what the client is saying and, if at all possible, be involved in preparing the message. By the same token, the lawyer's comments about courtroom proceedings may affect the client outside the courtroom in ways the lawyer cannot fully appreciate; therefore, the client needs to know and oversee what the lawyer is saying. Both goals suggest the need for constant lawyer-client communication regarding any media strategy.

Providing Necessary Facts

It has often been said that the media don't report the truth, they report facts; consequently, the best way to defend yourself from unfair attack is to ensure that the media know the counterfacts. This allows the media to evaluate the responsibility of the original attack, or to temper its sting by inclusion of the counterfacts in the story. Due to intimate knowledge of a case and the other side's arguments, the lawyer is often the best person to identify the facts necessary to blunt or sharpen the attack.

Nuts and Bolts

Before litigation even begins, both lawyer and client must be prepared for possible media attention. In assessing the likelihood of media interest in a case, the lawyer should understand that lawsuits tend to prompt news stories. This is because difficulties encountered by journalists in reporting on potentially damaging allegations or dealing with reluctant sources become much easier when the matter is filed in court. Outside litigation, many companies try to "kill" stories by silence. They may purport to be unavailable, offer a terse "No comment," or go on the attack and threaten inquiring media with lawsuits. Whether such tactics are ever ultimately beneficial is debatable. But it is clear that although a client's silence may deter some prelitigation stories, it is much less likely to do so once the dispute has breached the courthouse doors. The occurrence of litigation often indicates that there will be a story, and the real issue is how best to explain the dispute and make the media understand the client's position.

Effectively doing so requires knowledge of the case. Like judges and juries, the media in the typical case do no investigation on their own, but rely instead on the parties for an understanding of the pertinent facts and legal contentions. Marshaling these facts and contentions is always the responsibility of the lawyer and, in a case likely to garner media attention, must be a priority from the outset.

The lawyer needs to ensure that what is said to the media comports with the evidence expected to be developed in the proceeding. When the client will be the one speaking to the media, the lawyer should screen whatever will be said. Preparation is essential because the time for response is often short. First impressions are important, and a response of "No comment" often leaves the wrong one.

In preparing for and helping coordinate media comment, the lawyer should understand and explain to the client that not all media are alike and consider whether and how the proposed comment is likely to reach or affect the tribunal, be it a judge or jury.

Conclusion

For better or worse, media attention often is an important part of the litigation equation. The media may be the most important tool your client has for educating the public and building support for— or at least preventing unnecessary damage to—its position. Lawyers who fail to understand this and who neglect to help their clients in doing so are not engaging in effective representation.

Think Before You Leap: Talking to the Media

10

Paul Mark Sandler

IT IS A BUSY DAY. Matters intensify when your secretary interrupts, "WBAL-TV is on line 4, Channel 2 is on line 3, and, while you were on the phone, Tom Hendricks of *The Sun* and Jane Brett of *The Post* called. They want to speak to you immediately about the Casper case."

Well, you are in it now: You have a cause célèbre. Everyone wants to hear from you, but how do you deal with the press when you represent a client in a pending case? What do you say? When do you say it? What issues need your focus?

There are five points you should consider before responding to the media. But first, ask your secretary to advise WBAL-TV holding on line 4, and Channel 2 holding on line 3, that you will return the call in 20 minutes. Then, reflect on these following points before you utter one word to the media:

1. Know the ABA Model Rule and state guidelines relating to comments to the media.
2. Always protect your client's best interests—not your own interests—when commenting to the media about a case.

101

3. Think about what you wish to say before commenting, because an unintended remark to the media is always "fair game."

4. Develop appropriate phrases that you anticipate will interest the reporter, because if you do comment, you want your comment publicized. Frequently, reporters misunderstand your remark or editors delete your comments. What you thought you were communicating may not appear in the publication.

5. You must consider the judge, opposing counsel, and the strategy of what you are attempting to accomplish.

ABA Model Rule of Professional Conduct Relating to Trial Publicity, and State Guidelines

ABA Model Rule 3.6[1] prohibits counsel from making public statements that threaten a party's right to a fair trial. The Rule prevents counsel from commenting to the media if the lawyer knows that the statement will have a substantial likelihood of materially prejudicing the proceedings. Nevertheless, the Model Rule does permit counsel to state the following: (1) the claim, offense, or defense involved, (2) except when prohibited by law, the identity of the persons involved, (3) information contained in the public record, (4) notice that an investigation of a matter is in progress, (5) the scheduling or result of any step in litigation, (6) a request for assistance in obtaining evidence and information, (7) a warning of danger concerning behavior of a person involved when there is reason to believe that there exists the likelihood of harm to an individual or to the public interest, (8) in criminal cases, the identity, residence, occupation, and family status of the accused, (9) if the accused has not been apprehended, information necessary to aid in apprehension of that person, (10) the fact, time, and place of arrest, (11) the identity of investigating and arresting officers or agencies, and (12) the length of the investigation.

Significantly, the Model Rule allows a lawyer to make a statement that a reasonable lawyer would believe is necessary to protect the client from substantial prejudicial effects of recent publicity not initiated by the lawyer or the lawyer's client. The Rule provides that, before a lawyer can be disciplined for out-of-court statements, the lawyer must know that disseminating the statement has a substantial likelihood of prejudicing the proceedings, and that such prejudice is material. (The Supreme Court case of *Gentile v. State Bar of Nevada*,[2] prompted the ABA to revise its Model Rule.)

Not all jurisdictions have adopted the Model Rule. Therefore, you would be wise to consult the applicable provisions in the jurisdictions where you practice. (Also see Chapter 11 for a more thorough review of ethical guidelines.)

Your Client's Best Interests—Not Your Own

Despite the urge for fame and glory as a trial lawyer, in many instances you would be prudent to refrain from making any comments about your case to the media. Inappropriate comments can have a detrimental effect on the judge or jury. On the other hand, in some cases, comments to the media can have a profound and positive effect on a case. There may be times when your client needs to initiate or counteract publicity for reasons unrelated to what will happen in the courtroom. Nonetheless, publicity may well have an impact in the courtroom. (For example, some argue that in the O.J. Simpson case, the repeated out-of-court statements by defense counsel established a disposition by the jury to receive evidence of a police conspiracy more favorably.) When to present comments to the media and when to refrain is often a question of judgment.

Nevertheless, the urge to be quoted may threaten to overcome your better judgment that commenting is not in your client's interest. When that happens, bite your tongue. Remember to caution your client to refrain from comments as well, if they will interfere with the courtroom proceedings. Suggest to the client that he or she should consult with you before responding to any media contacts. It may be best for you to respond instead.

Foremost in your mind should be the client's best interests; and although every lawyer pays lip service to this standard, many talk to the media because they want to see their names in print.

This is regrettable, not only because counsel could inadvertently betray his or her client, but also because inappropriate statements to the press can jeopardize the lawyer's credibility with the court and opposing counsel.

Prepare First, Speak Later

When talking to reporters, whatever you say is quotable. Often times, calls from the media catch lawyers off guard. Many people have a tendency to ramble in response to a question without hitting the point directly. Most also have a natural tendency to think out loud, thus exposing to publication otherwise confidential or inappropriate ideas. Therefore, to be most effective, prepare a statement in advance, even if you think there is only a remote chance you will be contacted by the media.

Several other chapters in this book address preparation techniques in more detail; suffice it here to reiterate two main points: (1) make certain both you and the reporter have the same understanding of the meaning of "off the record," and (2) develop key words that you know will interest the reporter.

When giving interviews for radio and television, there is usually ample time to prepare. That is less likely when you exit the courthouse and members of the media gather about you. In those situations, it is important to have prepared remarks, but limited ones, to avoid "retrying the case in the media." The important consideration is to take control of the interview. Control is best gained by limiting your comments to what you intend to say and not being goaded into making further comments, particularly as you walk away.

Develop Articulate Expressions That Crystalize Your Message in an Invigorating Manner

What you say may or may not be quoted accurately. First, the reporter may misunderstand your comment. Second, the editor may change the article and delete what you think to be your most important point. Therefore, if you give a short, specific quote that you believe advances your position in a stylistic fashion, there is a greater likelihood of your remarks remaining intact. The longer you speak and the more you ramble, the more susceptible you are to mistakes borne of miscommunication with the reporter or poor edits in the rush of meeting deadlines and limitations of time (in broadcast) or space (in print).

Know the Attitudes of the Judge and Opposing Counsel

Notwithstanding the law or ethical guidelines, consider the climate in the courtroom and your relationship with the judge and opposing counsel when you make comments about your case to the media. You should expect that when you make remarks, the judge and opposing counsel will read them. As noted, sometimes your remarks can appear in a context other than the one you intended when you spoke to the reporter. To maintain credibility for you and your client, exercise self-restraint in what you say. Certainly, if the court informally suggests that counsel limit remarks, you must be careful to abide by the court's wishes, unless you particularly calculate that it is appropriate and necessary to exceed the bounds of those wishes. For example, if opposing counsel makes remarks you deem inappropriate, you may feel compelled to counter those remarks, even though the judge may not be pleased. If a gag order has been entered, however, the stakes are higher: a violation may result in a citation for contempt.

A Sample Interview

With the above considerations in mind, it is now time to return the phone call you received from WBAL-TV, Channel 2, and the newspapers. Here is how you might proceed:

Lawyer: Hi, Tom. How are you doing?

Reporter: I'm fine. Steve, can you comment on Judge Jones's decision to deny your motion on behalf of the councilperson to dismiss the Attorney General's complaint?

Lawyer: Well, Tom, let's go off the record for a minute—do you mind?

Reporter: Steve, why don't we talk on the record? I would like to get a quote from you.

Lawyer: Tom, I just can't do that now. If you want to talk, let's go off the record. Then maybe we can go back on the record. And by the way, when I say "off the record," I mean that I do not want any of my comments quoted, used without attribution, or used in any other way. Do we have an agreement on that meaning?

Reporter: Yes, we do. Now, off the record, why don't you tell me what's up?

Lawyer: Well, as you know, it's a matter of public record that we claim the court lacks jurisdiction to hear the Attorney General's complaint in this instance. The Attorney General seeks to disqualify the councilperson from serving as a duly elected official, because he did not satisfy the jurisdictional requirements of living in his district for one year before being elected. But, the Attorney General is incorrect in this instance. First, Councilperson Jones was living in his district for more than a year. The fact that he was not physically living at the designated residence is because he was a law student studying out of town. Second, the court lacks jurisdiction, because the Board of Election Supervisors did not rule administratively that the councilperson lacked the one-year residency requirement. Rather, the Board of Elections simply deferred to the Attorney General and asked the Attorney General to institute the lawsuit in circuit court. Our position is that because the Board of Election Supervisors did not actually make a decision, there is no case or controversy, and thus the court lacks jurisdiction.

Reporter: Steve, why can't you give me a quote on the record?

Lawyer: Well, Tom, here is my quote, on the record: I do not think it is appropriate to comment on the judge's specific ruling in this instance. We do believe that the court lacks jurisdiction, but the judge made his ruling. We are confident, however, that when the testimony unfolds, the court will conclude on the merits that the councilperson did, in fact, reside in his district for longer than a year.

Notice that the lawyer did not criticize the judge for ruling against the client. What would that accomplish? The lawyer needs the judge's sympathy. Nevertheless, the lawyer provided—off the record—his own view of the law. This background information will be helpful as the reporter follows the case. By developing rapport with the reporter, a lawyer may have success in influencing the reporter to be sympathetic to the cause.

It is critical to give careful thought to what will be said in the interview, so it may not be in your best interests (that is, your client's best interests) to take a reporter's call immediately. Gather your thoughts first. In the example, the lawyer did not speak on the record immediately upon returning the call, but chatted off the record to get acclimated to the phone call, to relax, to get the reporter listening to him, and to catch the reporter's attention when the lawyer was ready to offer a quote. By doing so, he maximized the chance that the desired message came through clearly, and in a manner most likely to make it into the newspaper or broadcast intact.

Endnotes

1. Model Rules of Professional Conduct Rule 36 (1999).
2. Gentile v. State Bar of Nevada, 501 U.S. 1030 (1991).

Ethical Responsibilities When Dealing with the Media

11

Anthony E. DiResta

THE PRACTICE OF LAW and interacting with the media seem to go hand-in-hand these days. Perhaps it is not something you confront each and every day. But once or twice in their careers, most litigators will have to deal with seeking out—or responding to—the media on behalf of a client.

Consider the following three scenarios:

1. You are working on a civil matter with a difficult client. The client, seeking to put pressure on your opponents, asks you to call a reporter to leak some embarrassing information contained in a pleading that you are just about to file.

2. You are involved in a criminal defense matter that is about to go to trial. The prosecutor has obvious political ambitions. You get a call from the local newspaper, which asks for a reply to statements from the prosecutor about your "outrageous" defense tactics.

3. You are a litigation partner in a law firm, representing a large institutional client in a criti-

cally important piece of litigation involving trade secrets. Having just left a stressful management meeting, you are informed, through a note on your chair, that one of your associates just received a call about the case from a reporter "working on deadline." A telephone message indicates that the reporter wants you to comment immediately about certain documents that obviously were leaked by opposing counsel.

Aside from reaching for the antacids, what are you to do? Assuming that a blanket, "No comment" is not an attractive option from your client's perspective, what ethical standards exist that govern your ability to speak to the media?

What's that? Ethical standards? For dealing with the media? Why do lawyers need to adhere to these standards when some reporters fall short of doing so? The relevant ethical rules, of course, have nothing to do with the media. They have everything to do with the courts in which lawyers practice and the justice system of which they are an essential part. Before giving the reporter an earful about that unethical prosecutor, that lying witness, or the despicable opposing party, know the limits on how far you can go.

Ethics Guidance: Where to Look

The Code of Professional Responsibility[1] and the Model Rules of Professional Conduct[2] have provisions governing trial publicity. The jurisdictions where you practice may have adopted one or the other of these sets of rules, or a variation thereof. Thus, you should study those rules closely to determine exactly what type of information can or cannot be provided to the media. In addition, consult the local rules of the court in which you are litigating. For example, the Local Rules for the Northern District of Georgia contain a provision concerning special orders in high-profile civil or criminal cases:

In a widely publicized or sensational civil or criminal case, the Court, on motion of either party or on its own motion, may issue a special order governing such matters as extra-judicial statements by parties and witnesses likely to interfere with the rights of the parties or the rights of the accused to a fair trial by an impartial jury. . . .[3]

Moreover, special provisions may exist in your jurisdiction concerning statements in a variety of contexts. Some examples of areas in which special rules may apply include these:

- Professional disciplinary proceedings
- Juvenile proceedings
- Domestic relations matters
- Mental disability proceedings

Finally, your position—particularly if you are employed by a governmental entity—may have a bearing on what you can state to the media. For example, special rules exist for prosecutors,[4] for U.S. Department of Justice personnel,[5] and for lawyers working for governmental agencies such as the Federal Trade Commission.[6]

The Guidelines

Publicity Involving Civil Matters

Acceptable

Lawyers can quote from, or refer reporters to, information contained in a public record. In addition, a lawyer may state the following:[7]

1. The claim, offense, or defense involved
2. The identity of the persons involved in the civil proceedings, except when prohibited by law
3. The fact that an investigation of a matter is pending
4. The scheduling or result of any step in litigation
5. A request for assistance in obtaining evidence
6. A warning of danger concerning the behavior of a person involved in the proceedings, when there is reason to believe that substantial harm to an individual or to the public interest exists

Unacceptable

On the other hand, lawyers *must avoid* statements about the following:[8]

1. Evidence surrounding the occurrence or transaction involved
2. The character, credibility, or criminal record of a party or witness
3. The results of any examinations or tests—or the refusal of a party to submit to an exam or test
4. The lawyer's opinion concerning the merits of the claims or defenses

Publicity Involving Criminal Matters

Acceptable

A lawyer associated with the investigation of a criminal matter may quote from or refer to the public record. In addition, the lawyer may state the following, without elaboration:[9]

1. That an investigation is in progress
2. The name, age, residence, occupation, and family status of the accused
3. The fact, time, and place of the arrest; resistance to the arrest; pursuit of the accused before the arrest; and the use of weapons
4. The identity of investigating and arresting officers or agencies, and the length of the investigation
5. At the time of the seizure, a description of the evidence seized—other than a confession, admission, or statement
6. The nature of the charge
7. The scheduling or result of any step in the judicial proceedings
8. That the accused denies the charges made against him or her
9. A description of the offense and, if permitted by law, the identity of the victim
10. A request for assistance in obtaining evidence

11. A request for assistance in apprehending a suspect
12. A warning to the public of any dangers

Unacceptable

On the other hand, lawyers *must avoid* statements about the following:[10]

1. The character, reputation, or prior criminal record of the accused
2. The possibility of a guilty plea to the offense charged or to a lesser offense
3. The existence of any confession, admission, or statement given by the accused—or his/her refusal or failure to make a statement
4. The performance or results of any examinations or tests (such as fingerprints, polygraphs, ballistic tests, or DNA testing)—or the refusal or failure of the accused to submit to an exam or test
5. The identity, testimony, or credibility of a prospective witness
6. Any opinion concerning the guilt or innocence of the accused, the evidence, or the merits of the case

Conclusion

Confidence in our legal system requires disputes to be resolved by an impartial tribunal. Yet, as demonstrated by the criminal and civil trials of O.J. Simpson, the pretrial publicity surrounding the Oklahoma City bombing, and the lawsuits by several Attorneys General against the tobacco companies, the goal of impartiality may be defeated by news or commentary that attempts to influence a judge, a jury, the witnesses—or even public opinion.

Trial publicity also can threaten the reputations of targeted parties, especially criminal defendants and defendants in civil actions brought under the Racketeer Influenced and Corrupt Organizations Act. In many instances, a "not guilty" or "not liable" verdict does not provide vindication. Many people assume the guilt of any person charged with a crime.

On the other hand, vital constitutional interests are served by the free dissemination of information. The public has a right to know information affecting its choices as consumers and roles as citizens. It has a right to know about any threats to safety and measures aimed at assuring security. The public also has a right to know about the conduct of judicial proceedings. As Justice Brennan articulated in 1980, the first amendment has a "structural role to play in securing and fostering our republican system of self-government."[11] Whether a judge is doing his or her job is critically important to the public when it comes time to elect or reelect these public officials.

As a result of the tension between the need to ensure a fair proceeding and the need to have access to information of public concern, ethics rules have been adopted to guide lawyers on their out-of-court statements to the media. The general principal is this: Avoid statements that are likely to interfere with a fair trial or, in the criminal context, that are likely to affect the imposition of a sentence. Remember that in each case, however, you must know your local rules to avoid running afoul of guidelines that may vary from the Model Rules.

Endnotes

1. MODEL CODE OF PROFESSIONAL RESPONSIBILITY DR 7-107 (1980).

2. MODEL RULES OF PROFESSIONAL CONDUCT Rule 3.6 (1999).

3. LOCAL RULES OF THE UNITED STATES DISTRICT COURT FOR THE NORTHERN DISTRICT OF GEORGIA 83.4(B).

4. *See* MODEL RULES OF PROFESSIONAL CONDUCT Rule 3.8 (1999).

5. *See* UNITED STATES DEPARTMENT OF JUSTICE, UNITED STATES ATTORNEY'S MANUAL §§ 1-7.000–1-7.700, 9-2.200–9-2.211 (1992).

6. *See, e.g.,* Clayton Act, Pub. L. No. 94-435, § 201, 90 Stat. 1393 (1976) (Current version at 15 U.S.C § 18a(h)) (1994) (Section 7A(h) of Clayton Act, which forbids disclosure of information obtained from premerger notification filings and second requests under Hart-Scott-Rodino Act).

7. MODEL CODE OF PROFESSIONAL RESPONSIBILITY DR 7-107(G) (1980); MODEL RULES OF PROFESSIONAL CONDUCT Rule 3.6(b) (1999).

8. MODEL RULES OF PROFESSIONAL CONDUCT Rule 3.6 cmt. [5] (1999).

9. MODEL CODE OF PROFESSIONAL RESPONSIBILITY DR 7-107(A), DR 7-107(C) (1980); MODEL RULES OF PROFESSIONAL CONDUCT Rule 3.6(b) (1999).

10. MODEL CODE OF PROFESSIONAL RESPONSIBILITY DR 7-107(B) (1980); MODEL RULES OF PROFESSIONAL CONDUCT Rule 3.6 cmt. [5] (1999).

11. Richmond Newspapers, Inc. v. Virginia, 448 U.S. 558, 587 (1990) (Brennan, J., concurring).

Prosecutors and the Media 12

Lee Stapleton Milford and Wilfredo Fernandez[1]

THE FEDERAL PROSECUTOR EMERGES from the courthouse. The jury has reached a verdict after a grueling six-week trial. All the defendants were found guilty as charged. Lights glaring harshly, a swarm of reporters thrust microphones in the face of the Assistant U.S. Attorney, shouting questions. The appropriate response? "We are pleased with the jury's verdict. Justice has been served."

Another federal prosecutor receives a verdict after an equally grueling trial. The verdict, across the board: not guilty. Same lights, same microphones. The appropriate response? "We are disappointed with the jury's verdict, but respect its decision."

Various rules constrain and circumscribe what a prosecutor can (and cannot) say publicly about a case, and the parameters of any remarks vary with the circumstances. A balance must be struck between protecting an individual's legal rights, and the public's right to know about the work of prosecutors paid from the public's funds.

There was a time when a chapter describing prosecutors and their relationships with the media could not fill more than one page. Times have changed. *Court TV* is part of our culture, and criminal trials are presented for all America to critique. And in an era when lawyers routinely take to the airwaves to discuss investigative and trial strategy, prosecutors must—for practical and policy reasons—understand the demands of the media, explain the use of government resources, and use restraint to communicate effectively with the public.

Limits on the Prosecutor

Grand Juries and Federal Rule 6(e)

It is difficult to turn on the television without hearing about grand juries and their mysterious work. The footage typically shows witnesses, often accompanied by their lawyers, entering and leaving the building where the federal grand jury sits. You will likely never see a prosecutor providing an impromptu interview on the courthouse steps after a day with the grand jury, and for good reason—such remarks would be illegal.

The Nature of the Limit, and Sanctions for Disregarding It

Federal law prohibits the government from releasing any information regarding the grand jury process. Federal Rule of Criminal Procedure 6(e) forbids the disclosure of matters occurring before the grand jury, and the rule applies the moment the first grand jury subpoena is issued. The rule does not contemplate the release of such information to the media under *any circumstances*. In fact, the government's confirmation of the existence of a grand jury investigation may violate this rule. A knowing violation can be punished as a contempt of court.

In most instances, leaks of grand jury information trigger investigations by the Office of Professional Responsibility (OPR)—the U.S. Department of Justice's "internal affairs" division. Information regarding a grand jury investigation or sealed proceedings that are attributed to a "government or law enforcement" source usually guarantees an OPR investigation of those who might have leaked information, and can subject a prosecutor to court sanctions and/or bar complaints.

The Secrecy Requirement

The grand jury process is designed to allow the government an opportunity to investigate, purportedly in secret, to allow facts to develop fully before a target who may not be guilty of anything is besmirched. With the possible exception of publicly traded companies for whom Securities and Exchange Commission regulations require disclosure of being named a "subject" or "target" of a grand jury investigation, the entire process is designed to be kept secret. Secrecy extends not only to grand jury testimony, but also to the identity of witnesses called before the grand jury and documents produced to the grand jury. The only people allowed in the grand jury room are lawyers for the government, the witness under examination, interpreters when needed, and a stenographer or operator of a recording device.

Although those who are in front of the grand jury on official business—grand jurors, prosecutors, agents, and stenographers—are bound by the secrecy requirement, no such rule binds those who testify in front of the grand jury. Should a witness be so inclined, he or she may leave the grand jury room and immediately discuss every aspect of his or her testimony with the world. As a recent *Washington Post* editorial succinctly stated, "the federal rules of criminal procedure permit grand jury witnesses and targets to gab all they like about what they have said in the grand jury room. The secrecy requirements are designed to protect innocent people from having their names dragged through the mud, not to keep the witnesses themselves from talking."[2]

The identities of grand jurors are not made public. Recently, however, witnesses who testified in front of a Washington grand jury and heard evidence in a high-profile case discussed the characteristics of the grand jurors with the press; apparently the fact that the majority of the grand jurors were women and that they did not dress particularly well was considered worthy of a newspaper article. The witnesses also noted that at times the grand jurors seemed disinterested in the testimony, and walked in and out of the grand jury room while testimony was being given. Certainly the grand jurors themselves could not have discussed "a day in the life of a grand juror," but there was no such prohibition on the witnesses who observed the grand jurors doing their work.

Post-Indictment Stage: The U.S. Attorney's Manual, Federal Regulations, and Local Court Rules

Once the grand jury completes its work, the grand jurors either (1) conclude that the targets may have run afoul of the law and return an indictment, or (2) conclude that no crime was committed. The indictment is a charging document prepared by the prosecutor, which sets forth the nature of the violations charged. The grand jury votes on the indictment, and if it agrees that there is probable cause to believe that crimes have been committed, the targets are indicted and become criminal defendants.

The U.S. Attorney's Manual

The U.S. Attorney's Manual (USAM) sets forth—with great particularity—what information can be released regarding an indictment.[3] Weight is given to protecting the rights of the victims and litigants, as well as protecting the life and safety of other parties and witnesses. The rules allow only basic information about a matter to be released. In a criminal case in which charges have been brought, the following information may be released:

1. The defendant's name, age, residence, employment, marital status, and similar background information
2. The substance of the charge, limited to that contained in the complaint, indictment, information, or other public documents
3. The identity of the investigating and/or arresting agency and the length and scope of an investigation
4. The circumstances immediately surrounding an arrest, including the time and place of an arrest, resistance, pursuit, possession and use of weapons, and a description of the physical items seized at the time of arrest

These disclosures cannot include subjective observations, but the public policy significance of a case may be discussed. Law enforcement agencies involved in an investigation are subject to the same restrictions. The USAM requires any Justice Department component—indeed, any agency involved in a Justice Department investigation—to coordinate with the local U.S. Attorney's Office before contacting the media.[4]

Federal Regulations

The USAM incorporates a federal regulation, which advocates that statements made by U.S. Justice Department personnel be "minimal" and that disclosures include "only incontrovertible, factual matters, and [not] subjective observations."[5]

Another federal regulation prohibits the release of midtrial statements.[6] Although it contemplates the release of information that is part of the public record, it does not permit dissemination of matters that would in any manner "interfere with a fair trial or otherwise prejudice the due administration of justice."[7] It is therefore inappropriate to inject commentary about criminal and civil proceedings through extrajudicial means—that means midtrial courthouse-step press conferences are not permitted. Though prosecutors may announce criminal charges at the onset of a case (arrest and indictment, for example), once the case is underway, they are generally prohibited from discussing most aspects of a pending court matter except those matters that are clearly in the public record. Prosecutors in most jurisdictions are never permitted to discuss the existence or contents of a confession or statement by the accused, the possibility of a plea agreement, or opinions about the merits of a case.

Local Court Rules

Local rules of court, which govern both civil and criminal proceedings at the federal level, are enacted and modified by district court judges. Though these rules generally cover font size and other technical requirements of pleadings, some also cover the extent to which information on a pending criminal case can be released. For example, in the Southern District of Florida, prosecutors and defense lawyers are forbidden to make "extrajudicial statements which a reasonable person would expect to be disseminated by means of public communications."[8]

Other Ways for the Media to Obtain Information

Due to the extent of limits placed on prosecutors, the media may not be able to obtain from them all the information it wants. The media can, however, acquire material in many other ways.

Speaking Indictments

A member of the media presented with a so-called "bare-bones" indictment will not have much to report. That document contains only the various "counts" of the indictment—the date and time of the alleged offense, tracking of the pertinent statutory language, and the statute being charged. Oftentimes, however, prosecutors prepare a "speaking indictment," which sets forth in greater detail the factual basis for what is being charged, as well as the overt acts of the criminal violation.

The Courtroom

Though prosecutors may be constrained about what they can say to the media, the courtroom is a different matter. For members of the media and others who have an urge to learn what a criminal case is really like, the courtroom is the place to be.

Initial Court Appearance

The first opportunity, soon after arrest, is the defendant's initial court appearance before the magistrate, when a determination of what bond, if any, is necessary to insure the defendant's appearance at subsequent court proceedings. At this time, the Assistant U.S. Attorney handling the case often provides a recitation of the criminal acts charged.

For instance, an indictment that charges a defendant with importing cocaine may be a one- or two-page document. In court, the prosecutor will likely outline that the defendant has been under investigation for 18 months by the Drug Enforcement Administration, the U.S. Customs Service, and the Internal Revenue Service. The prosecutor might reveal that the evidence at trial will consist of the testimony of an undercover informant, recorded conversations involving the importation of 500 kilograms of cocaine into the United States from Colombia, and videotape evidence of cocaine being off-loaded at a local warehouse, ostensibly as part of the defendant's frozen-food import/export business. To establish that the defendant is both a danger to the community and a flight risk as required under The Bail Reform Act,[9] the prosecutor might also proffer that at the time of the defendant's arrest, federal agents found false passports for him and his wife, as well as $100,000 in cash. These types of facts, which are an integral part of a standard pretrial detention hearing, also make interesting copy for the morning newspaper. Learning why the government believes a person presents a risk of flight (ties to other countries, large amounts of cash, or hidden assets, for example) or seeing who comes forward to speak on a defendant's behalf provides much insight into the case.

Hearing on a Motion to Suppress Evidence

In the weeks and months following the indictment, there will be many court appearances. Typically, the average criminal defendant files a motion to suppress evidence, on the grounds that evidence the government intends to use was illegally obtained. In most circumstances, an evidentiary hearing is held, during which the government presents witnesses and introduces evidence. The hearing on a motion to suppress evidence offers a good preview of a trial, of both the government's evidence and the defense's strategy.

Change-of-Plea Hearing

In a multidefendant case, one or more defendants may decide to plead guilty. Change-of-plea hearings are, of course, open to the public; they provide an opportunity to hear both the government's view about an individual defendant and the scope of the government's case, because the government must present facts before a defendant's guilty plea. Some federal district court judges ask the defendants themselves to describe the facts surrounding the charges (to provide an appropriate factual basis for the plea as well as avoid the issue on appeal). Change-of-plea hearings also may be a signal that one of the codefendants is cooperating with the government.

Sentencing Hearing

Sentencing hearings offer opportunities to learn information that many times is not deemed admissible at trial. For instance, a defendant's prior criminal history, replete with details, is disclosed at sentencing, though such information would cause a mistrial if mentioned at trial.

The Court File

Reporters seeking more information as a case progresses periodically should check the court file. Often pleadings provide a road map for those interested in the interaction between defense and government lawyers. Pleadings may contain a wealth of factual information about the case, the defendant, and the defense motions about the weaknesses or perceived unfairness of the government's case.

As part of the case investigation, the court may have signed search warrants and wire-intercept applications. Affidavits must be filed in support of requests to obtain these items. During litigation, these affidavits are often unsealed and made public, and reveal a great deal about events that occurred during the course of the investigation.

Inferences and conclusions can be drawn from sealed pleadings as well. For instance, if a defendant has pled guilty and is cooperating, the plea agreement will be part of the court file, but sealed. These sealed pleadings warrant a question, even one that may not be answered.

Conclusion

Though in many situations federal or state law requires prosecutors to find the back door of the courthouse, today's prosecutor has an obligation to explain the government's posture on any given matter. Anyone who has lived through the horrors of Oklahoma City, Ruby Ridge, or Waco, realizes that explaining the government's conduct and the underlying policy for its decisions is imperative. In cases that attract national attention, the U.S. Justice

Department has historically appointed a representative from the Office of Public Affairs to field questions from the media and allow the prosecutors to focus on the criminal matter at hand, while keeping the public informed when it needs reassurance. The right of the people in a constitutional democracy to have access to information about the conduct of law enforcement officers, prosecutors, and the court is paramount.

Endnotes

1. The views expressed in this chapter are the authors', and not necessarily the position or views of the Department of Justice.

2. Editorial, *Grand Jury Secrecy,* WASH. POST, Feb. 8, 1998, at C6.

3. 1 UNITED STATES DEPARTMENT OF JUSTICE, U.S. ATTORNEY'S MANUAL § 1-7.000 (1997).

4. *Id.* § 7.520.

5. 28 C.F.R. § 50.2 (1997).

6. *Id.* § 50.2(2).

7. *Id.*

8. LOCAL RULES FOR THE UNITED STATES DISTRICT COURT FOR THE SOUTHERN DISTRICT OF FLORIDA 77.2(2)

9. 18 U.S.C. § 3142 (1984).

Dealing with the Media in a High-Profile Criminal Case

13

Ronald G. Woods

INCREASINGLY, federal criminal defense lawyers find themselves being asked to represent clients who the media—with the cooperation of "anonymous federal law enforcement sources"—have already "demonized," making it nearly impossible for such clients to receive a fair trial. Several high-profile cases serve as examples of this unfortunate trend:

♦ The Atlanta Olympic Games bombing allegation against Richard Jewell

♦ The Oklahoma City Federal Building bombing allegations against Timothy McVeigh and Terry Nichols

♦ The Ruby Ridge shootout and murder allegations against Randy Weaver

♦ The Unabomber allegations against Theodore Kaczynski

♦ The Branch Davidian murder allegations against the few remaining survivors of the assault and fire in Waco

In many such cases, federal law enforcement officers respond to the crime, make arrests, and immediately start cooperating with the media to feed them the kind of valuable information that is sought by competing journalists and media organizations in national, high-profile, attention-grabbing cases. Usually, the law enforcement agencies believe the publicity benefits them also, except in cases like the ones involving Richard Jewell (in which incriminating information was leaked against an innocent person), and Ruby Ridge and the Branch Davidians (in which the jury subsequently acquitted the defendants of the murder charges).

Law enforcement officials are certainly aware of the rules, regulations, and policies that govern their contacts with the media in criminal cases. That is why bland and innocuous statements appear when the organization's media spokesperson is being quoted by name, while the "anonymous federal law enforcement officials" are quoted giving the inflammatory, incriminating, highly prejudicial information that the media often emphasizes much more prominently.

The Rules

Federal prosecutors supervising the investigations and Department of Justice officials have a responsibility to ensure that the agencies follow the rules, regulations, guidelines, and policies of the U.S. Department of Justice as stated in federal regulations and the U.S. Attorney's Manual.[1] (See Chapter 11 for other discussions about the manual and federal regulations.)

The U.S. Attorney's Manual

The U.S. Attorney's Manual states as follows:

> In instances where field officers of any division or component (Federal Bureau of Investigation, Drug Enforcement Agency, Immigration and Naturalization Service, Bureau of Prisons, United States Marshals Service, United States Attorneys Offices and all Department of Justice Divisions)

plan to issue a news release, schedule a news conference or *make contact with a member of the media relating to any case or matter which may be prosecuted by the United States Attorney's office,* such release, scheduling of a news conference or other media contact *shall be approved by the United States Attorney.*[2]

This rule is honored in its breach rather than its observance. When media representatives arrive on the scene of a national high-profile case, they have little trouble developing "anonymous federal law enforcement sources" who provide them with highly prejudicial, inflammatory information, such as the results of tests and examinations, the contents of statements and admissions, and the nature of the defendant's character and prior criminal record, as well as other items that can prejudice the defendant and help assure a conviction.

Local Rules of Court

This type of conduct also violates local rules of the federal district courts, all of which have adopted the Free Press/Fair Trial Guidelines of the Judicial Conference of the United States[3] as part of their local rules governing disclosure and publicity in criminal cases. The guidelines prohibit a lawyer or law firm from releasing— or authorizing the release of—information or opinions that a reasonable person would expect to be disseminated by any means of public communication, in connection with pending or imminent criminal litigation with which a lawyer or law firm is associated, if there is a reasonable likelihood that such dissemination will interfere with a fair trial or otherwise prejudice the due administration of justice. Federal prosecutors and the law enforcement agents with whom they work in connection with criminal litigation are certainly governed by this rule.

The Model Rules of Professional Conduct

In addition, the American Bar Association Model Rules of Professional Conduct state as follows:

The prosecutor in a criminal case shall:

. . .

(e) exercise reasonable care to prevent investigators, law enforcement personnel, employees or other persons assisting or associated with the prosecutor in a criminal case from making an extrajudicial statement that the prosecutor would be prohibited from making under Rule 3.6.[4]

Responding to "Demonization" of Your Client

Given that these situations exist and given that the "demonization" is usually done within the first week after an incident occurs, most often before a criminal defense lawyer is asked to represent a client, how do you deal with the problem and how do you deal with the media?

Each case has different fact situations that influence how you proceed. If you are asked to represent someone who is unjustly accused (like Richard Jewell) and federal law enforcement authorities engage in speculation, you properly go on the offensive—talk with the media on and off the record to attempt to convince them of the error of the federal law enforcement officials and the innocence of your client. Your goal is to have the tenor of the media coverage more balanced, and eventually to help vindicate your client in the eyes of the public. This is not easy. As former Secretary of Labor Raymond Donovan said after being acquitted on corruption charges, "Where do I go to get my reputation back?"[5] It is a rare occasion when you can cause the media to reverse a demonization process and report complete vindication.

Most high-profile cases end up with charges being filed, and with you facing a trial when overwhelming negative publicity has already occurred. If the alleged crime is particularly heinous, you will often find that some members of the media and the "anonymous federal law enforcement sources" have formed a loose bond; this puts the burden of proof on the defendant and his or her lawyer to come forward with any evidence or information to ameliorate the tenor of the publicity surrounding the case. Law enforcement sources sometimes give the media the information they want presented, and the media reports the government's version verbatim. Some defense lawyers believe that in cases of this nature, media representatives lose their impartiality and act as advocates for the government when reporting the case.

Personal Experience:
The Oklahoma City Bombing Allegations

I served as appointed co-counsel representing Terry Nichols in the Oklahoma City Federal Building bombing allegations. This case shows what a lawyer can expect in a high-profile matter involving a client who is immediately "demonized" by some in the media, with the assistance of "anonymous federal law enforcement sources."

Early Media Coverage

Like all U.S. citizens, I was horrified to see the television coverage on April 19, 1995, including the bombed federal building in Oklahoma City and the deceased and injured people who were in the building. The national interest intensified on April 21, 1995, when Timothy McVeigh was taken into federal custody in Perry, Oklahoma, and charged with the bombing. He was taken to Oklahoma City to stand trial for the crime. Some in the media also reported that Terry Nichols voluntarily turned himself in to the Federal Bureau of Investigation (FBI) in Herington, Kansas, on April 21, 1995, and was arrested as a material witness.

Over the next several weeks, some media sources quoted "anonymous federal law enforcement officials" who provided alleged details of the backgrounds of McVeigh and Nichols, incriminating statements that both had allegedly made, and results of chemical and fingerprint tests from items seized from McVeigh and from a search of Nichols's home. The officials provided an alleged motive that these were two drifters and members of the militia, who were seeking revenge for the deaths of the Branch Davidians who were killed on April 19, 1993. The above-cited rules, regulations, and guidelines clearly list all this material as information that federal law enforcement officials are prohibited from disclosing. As a lawyer practicing in the federal criminal justice system, I felt outraged that federal law enforcement officials seemed to be doing so much to prejudice the defendants' rights to fair trials.

On May 9, 1995, Terry Nichols was formally charged with the commission of the crime and was transferred from Kansas to Oklahoma City to stand trial. A few days later, Mike Tigar and I were appointed co-counsel to represent Nichols, and the case then became much more personal—I had to do everything possible to assure that Terry Nichols received a fair trial.

Responding to Constant Media Requests

From the moment the appointment was announced, all the major print and television news organizations that were covering the case requested interviews. In high-profile cases, requests from the media never abate, from arrest and pretrial through trial and verdict. If you decide to make a statement, you must control when— and under what conditions—you will do so. We decided that we wanted to learn everything we could about the case before we made any public statement, if then.

Stopping the Leaks

In cases such as this, the first thing you want to accomplish is to shut down—or at least minimize—the continuous leaking by the "anonymous federal law enforcement officials." (Most federal prosecutors assigned to handle high-profile cases are conscientious and aware of the rules, regulations, and guidelines, and will not engage in prohibited conduct. They are also aware of leaking by others, and know they are responsible in court for the conduct of others.) We traveled to Oklahoma City and immediately asked for a meeting with the federal prosecutors handling the case. We gave them copies of various news articles, noting the numerous violations of rules, regulations, and guidelines by the quoted "anonymous federal law enforcement sources." We were assured by the prosecutors that the leaked stories "were hurting us more than you," that an internal investigation concerning the leaks was being conducted, and that they would give their best efforts to see that the leaks stopped.

We discovered later that their concern at that time was that the lawyer for Michael Fortier, a defendant who was negotiating with the government for reduced charges in exchange for his testimony, was about to withdraw his offer because the "anonymous federal law enforcement officials" were leaking to the press the details of his ongoing negotiations and the details of Fortier's proposed testimony. (Occasionally, actions by law enforcement personnel that prejudice a defendant's right to a fair trial backfire on them and the prosecutors.)

Compiling Samples of Media Coverage for a Motion to Change Venue

While in Oklahoma City, we quickly realized it would be impossible to receive a fair trial in the city or the state because of the intense negative publicity and the public statements of the U.S. president, the attorney general, the governor, the district attorney, and the "anonymous federal law enforcement sources." One of our first tasks was to start a compilation of all media coverage, including all news articles and television coverage, which we would use in our motion for a change of venue.

During this period, the lawyer for Timothy McVeigh had decided to conduct a media campaign to humanize his client. Although the media coverage did put a more benign face on McVeigh's image—to counter the government's image of the "perp walk," with McVeigh being led out of the Perry, Oklahoma, courthouse in an orange suit and shackles and surrounded by FBI agents—the contents of the articles and television coverage only reemphasized McVeigh's alleged role in the offense. The attempt at humanizing McVeigh led to more leaking by the "anonymous federal law enforcement sources" and very quickly the coverage escalated as one side after the other made statements to the media.

Deciding to Refrain from Comment

Though we continued to be inundated with media requests for interviews, client interviews, and statements on and off the record, we believed that refraining from comment served the best interests of our client. Media coverage had shifted to McVeigh alone and Terry Nichols was quickly moved to the background. Inasmuch as we sensed it would be a lengthy period before we reached trial, we felt the best course was to allow the public to forget Nichols while media coverage focused on McVeigh. By the time we started trial in September 1997, this was proven to be the right course.

After presentation of evidence in a hearing on the motion to change venue, the court stated as follows:

> The intensity of the humanization of the victims is in sharp contrast with the prevalent portrayals of the defendants. They have been demonized. . . . Upon all of the evidence presented, this Court finds and concludes that there is so great a prejudice against these two defendants in the State of Oklahoma that they cannot obtain a fair and impartial trial at any place fixed by law for holding court in that State.[6]

The case was moved to Denver, a severance was granted, and Timothy McVeigh was tried first. During this period, we continued to have no comment on behalf of Terry Nichols. After the trial, conviction, and death sentence for McVeigh, and all the attendant publicity, we did not believe we could find an impartial jury in Denver. However, from conducting a short poll and going into individual voir dire, we discovered that the average citizen in the area was very unfamiliar with Terry Nichols, did not know what he was specifically accused of, and had not made decisions based on any media coverage.

We believe that the policy of not commenting on the case helped assure a fair trial for our client. In our limited contact with the media from May 1995 until the verdict on lesser charges was returned in January 1998, we found that a majority of the media, because of the nature of the case, had lost impartiality and were advocates for the prosecution. In the few instances when we noted the contradictions and errors in past reporting and summarizing of the case, we felt as though we were dealing with adversaries rather than impartial reporters of facts.

The lesson learned was that when you face negative and hostile media because of the nature of the case, and you have a way to deflect the attention of the media from your client, take it. The public, which is your potential jury pool, quickly forgets about a defendant over passage of time. Because our obligation is to secure a fair trial for the client, passing the opportunity to be part of the media coverage of a high-profile case may be the best way to secure a fair trial and an unbiased jury.

Presenting Media Issues to the Court

If your client is the only defendant in a case and the media and "anonymous federal law enforcement officials" are engaging in demonization, try to make that work to your advantage with the trial judge. Begin compiling all news articles and television coverage concerning your client. This can be done by a newsclipping service, your law clerks, paralegals, or members of the defendant's family. Take a sampling from all media sources and make a formal presentation to the prosecutors handling the case, citing the above rules and regulations, and insist that the prejudicial leaking cease. Copy this formal presentation to the court and to the U.S. Attorney General.

You may find that this protest has little effect on the continuous leaking to the media. As Director Louie Freeh of the FBI stated, after the FBI did a "thorough" investigation of the leaks in the Richard Jewell case, he "had no reason to believe the leak came from the FBI."[7] Agents within law enforcement agencies and officials at the U.S. Department of Justice are aware that the news media will resist efforts to reveal confidential sources and that they can often leak information with virtual immunity.

As soon as you have examples of the continuing leaking, start filing the appropriate motions with the trial judge or the judge supervising the grand jury. Needless to say, the defense lawyer must have "clean hands" when he or she is making the appropriate complaints to the judge. If the defense lawyer has responded to this sudden exposure to the limelight by appearing on all the talk shows and by giving multiple interviews, the judge will have little reason to consider the complaints seriously.

Most federal judges try to ensure that the defendant receives a fair trial. If you present the government's "demonization" to the court with clean hands, you may obtain sanctions against the government and/or a change of venue. If the judge does nothing, you will at least be in a position where you cannot be easily criticized for your subsequent public comments attempting to level the playing field.[8]

Endnotes

1. *See* 28 C.F.R. § 50.2 (1999); UNITED STATES DEPARTMENT OF JUSTICE, U.S. ATTORNEYS' MANUAL § 1-7.000 (1997).

2. *Id.* at § 1-7.420 (emphasis added).

3. 87 F.R.D. 519, 525 (E.D. Wisc. 1980).

4. MODEL RULES OF PROFESSIONAL CONDUCT Rule 3.8 (1999) (Special Responsibilities of a Prosecutor).

5. NEW YORK TIMES, May 26, 1987, at A1.

6. 918 F.Supp. 1467 (W.D. Okla. 1996).

7. Associated Press, July 30, 1977.

8. *See* Gentile v. State Bar of Nevada, 501 U.S. 1030 (1991).

Unpopular Clients or Causes and the Media

14

Jeffrey O. Bramlett and Paul H. Schwartz

Representing the Unpopular: Rising to the Professional Challenge

"History is replete with instances of distinguished and sacrificial services by lawyers who have represented unpopular clients and causes."[1] Even before the birth of the nation, John Adams and Josiah Quincy, Jr., weathered the angry storm of public opinion aroused by their defense of the British soldiers accused of murdering five colonists in the so-called Boston Massacre.[2] Earlier this century, Clarence Darrow represented numerous "pariah" clients, from Eugene Debs, the Socialist union leader, to Nathan Leopold and Richard Loeb, the wealthy Chicagoans accused of murdering a 14-year-old boy, to John T. Scopes, the schoolteacher indicted for teaching evolution in Tennessee. Montgomery, Alabama, native Clifford Durr fought the injustices of his time and of the white Southern society from which he came, defending accused communists and both blacks and whites devoted to the cause of civil rights in the 1950s and

1960s. Examples of courageous lawyering abound, in cases both long forgotten and not soon to be forgotten.

In cases involving an unpopular client or cause, lawyers confront the special challenges presented by the intense media coverage, public scrutiny, and torrent of emotions such cases naturally inspire. Consider Adams's and Quincy's defense of sequential, separate trials of Captain Preston and the troops under his command for their respective roles in the Boston Massacre. Preston was tried first in a political atmosphere charged by the wide dissemination of an inflammatory report, dramatically entitled, "A Short Narrative of the horrid Massacre in Boston, perpetrated in the evening of the fifth day of March, 1770, by soldiers of the Twenty-ninth Regiment . . . with some observations on the state of things prior to that catastrophe."[3] When Adams and Quincy won Preston's acquittal, the *Boston Gazette* went even further in calling for vengeance against Preston's troops:

> Is it a dream,—murder on the 5th of March, with the dogs greedily licking human blood in King-Street? Some say that righteous Heaven will avenge it. And what says the Law of God, Whoso sheddeth Man's blood, by Man shall his Blood be shed![4]

Like Captain Preston, the British soldiers prevailed despite the *Gazette's* pretrial verdict. In the early part of this century, Leo Frank of Atlanta was not so fortunate. In 1913, Frank, the Jewish part-owner of a pencil factory, was charged with the murder of a young girl at the factory. With blatant anti-Semitism,

> [t]he three daily newspapers leapt upon the crime with an indecent, voyeuristic sensationalism of a sort very familiar to late-twentieth-century magazine readers and TV viewers. The public's appetite for lurid details, and for justice, was boundless: newspaper circulation skyrocketed with slanderous reports of this archetypal southern crime. Accounts of the trial referred to the defendant as "the monster" and "the strangler."[5]

After a trial in which angry mobs responded to newspaper editorials about the "jewpervert" by bombarding the courtroom with demands for a guilty verdict, Frank was convicted and sentenced to death. In 1915, when Georgia Governor John M. Slaton courageously commuted Frank's death sentence because of the gross unfairness of the trial proceedings, a band of 25 men, including 2 former state supreme court justices, kidnapped Frank from his prison cell and hanged him from a tree.[6]

Arthur Kinoy presents us with a third example in recounting his efforts to stay the executions of convicted "atomic spies" Julius and Ethel Rosenberg at the height of anticommunist hysteria in 1951.[7] Arguing before Second Circuit Judge Jerome Frank at his home in a desperate attempt to block electrocutions scheduled to proceed in less than six hours, Kinoy describes the result of his advocacy:

> At last we were finished. We had been talking and arguing for more than an hour. We looked up at him, and [Judge Frank] looked at us and was quiet for a moment. Then he said something that I shall never forget. He said to us in soft, slow words, "If I were as young as you are, I would be sitting where you are right now and saying and arguing what you are arguing. You are right to do so. But when you are as old as I am, you will understand why I"—and he paused, and repeated—"why I cannot do what you ask. I cannot do it."[8]

Lawyers' Roles and Objectives When Interacting with the Media

These cases illustrate some of the recurring difficulties in representing unpopular causes or clients. Achieving justice for the unpopular is always an upstream swim, because the law and those who administer it have a tendency (like most human beings and human institutions) to produce results that please the public. In high-profile cases, this tilt in the playing field is exacerbated as each participant—witness, juror, judge, and lawyer—experiences the glare of public scrutiny expressing, reinforcing, and serving as a reminder to all of the public will. Lawyers, who tend to be a competitive lot, generally hate to lose, especially when everyone is watching. Yet, in representing the unpopular client or cause, the risk of a painful public loss is always present.

Having acknowledged these realities, what are the lawyer's legitimate roles and objectives when interacting with the media in these cases? When law enforcement authorities parade a suspect in a notorious criminal case before cameras in jail garb and chains, does "no comment" from the suspect's advocate suffice as a public response? When public officials embroiled in a high-profile dispute over the civil rights of prisoners, gays and lesbians, immigrants, or flagburners offer public justification for their positions by appealing to public sentiment against these unpopular groups, can the opposing advocate responsibly ignore these out-of-court arguments that shape public perception and policy—not to mention juror predisposition—about the client and the cause?

If one crosses this threshold to the conclusion that out-of-court communication to the public through the media, shaped (if not delivered) by the advocate, is essential to balance the scales and secure for the client a fighting chance to prevail, options proliferate. Should the message stress the content of the client's cause, or the process values advanced by a justice system that accords the respect of a fair trial even to the unpopular, or perhaps a combination of both? The judgment calls about how, and what, and when to communicate will vary from case to case, but should proceed from a fundamental, personal examination: Why am I advocating this unpopular client or cause in the first place?

Self-examination is the appropriate starting point because journalists are (or should be) intent on information that is accurate. This predisposes them toward focused and credible sources of information. Lawyers who have not gone through the exercise of examining their own motives are unlikely to persuade journalists that they are focused and credible sources of reliable information.

Formulating a Rationale for the Representation

One might begin the explanation with the concept of a lawyer's professional responsibility. The 1958 Report of the American Bar Association (ABA) and Association of American Law Schools Joint Conference on Professional Responsibility, for example, states that "[o]ne of the highest services the lawyer can render to society is to appear in court on behalf of clients whose causes are in disfavor with the general public."[9] The ABA's Model Code of Professional Responsibility makes the point even more forcefully: "Regardless of his personal feelings, a lawyer should not decline representation because a client or a cause is unpopular or community reaction is adverse."[10]

Of course, reality and self-interest often clash with this ideal. Lawyers frequently are vilified for representing interests that the public at large, rightly or wrongly, views as immoral. Fifty years after his defense of the British soldiers, John Adams still felt the sting of popular condemnation: "At the present day it is impossible to realize the excitement of the populace, and the abuse heaped upon Mr. Quincy and myself for our defense of the British captain and his soldiers: we heard our names execrated in the most opprobrious terms whenever we appeared in the streets of Boston."[11] Not so long ago, David Goldberger and the American Civil Liberties Union suffered a similar flood of criticism, punctuated by massive membership resignations and even threats of physical violence, when they agreed to advocate the First Amendment rights of American Nazis to march in the predominantly Jewish community of Skokie, Illinois.[12] Lawyers representing death-row inmates regularly are excoriated and frequently driven to (or beyond) the brink of financial ruin for their pains.

Moreover, even if abstract references to professional responsibility satisfy the lawyer's inquiry, they may ring a bit hollow and unpersuasive to a public audience. Outraged at the client's alleged conduct or cause, members of the public demand to know of the lawyer: "Must *you* be the Devil's advocate?"[13] In the absence of a message incorporating a focused defense strategy and an emphasis on process values, ethical platitudes are not likely to satisfy this curiosity.

Advancing the Rationale: An Obligation?

Professional Ethics

Do lawyers have an obligation to justify to the public their representation of unpopular clients or causes? No easy answer lies in the rules of ethics. The ABA's Model Code and Model Rules of Professional Responsibility neither impose on lawyers a burden of publicly justifying their representation of particular clients, nor say explicitly that no obligation of public justification exists. At least one scholar has suggested that several ethical rules cut directly against the notion of a burden of public justification.[14] Presumably, this statement refers to, for example, the lawyer's obligations to preserve the confidences and secrets of the client[15] and to represent the client zealously within the bounds of the law,[16] since in the process of justifying oneself to the public, the lawyer may reveal information or impressions about the case, or even reinforce the public's negative view about the client, to the client's detriment.

But these ethical considerations are more appropriately viewed as *limitations* on the ability of a lawyer publicly to justify representation of a particular client, rather than absolute prohibitions against the lawyer doing so. To be sure, regardless of public scorn or demand for answers, a lawyer may not undermine the confidential nature of the attorney-client relationship, nor act in any way that is detrimental to the client. But often some kind of explanation for the representation can be given without compromising any ethical principles. In such a case, must the lawyer representing an unpopular client or cause publicly defend his or her decision to take on the client?

The answer depends largely on how the individual views his or her relationship to society as a lawyer. The unpopular client is unpopular generally because he stands for (or is perceived to stand for) some conduct or principle that the public views as immoral. Do we, as lawyers, have responsibility for the moral (or immoral) decisions of our clients? As lawyers in this society, do we have a *moral* obligation to justify our representation of a client perceived to be immoral?

Debate about Public Justification

A recent debate about whether lawyers have a burden of public justification centers on just these questions. In 1993, Professor Michael E. Tigar, then of the University of Texas School of Law (who represented accused Oklahoma City bombing accomplice Terry Lynn Nichols), undertook the representation of John Demjanjuk. Demjanjuk had been extradited to Israel in the 1980s to stand trial as "Ivan the Terrible" of Treblinka, one of the worst mass murderers of the Holocaust. Ultimately, the Israeli Supreme Court reversed Demjanjuk's conviction and death sentence based on the discovery of evidence—which the U.S. government apparently had withheld—that Demjanjuk was not Ivan the Terrible, but rather Ivan Marchenko, a guard at other Nazi concentration camps. Tigar agreed to assist Demjanjuk in his attempt to have his U.S. citizenship restored.

In what amounted to an open letter published in the *Legal Times,* Professor Monroe Freedman asked Tigar:

> [I]s John Demjanjuk the kind of client to whom you want to dedicate your training, your knowledge, and your extraordinary skills as a lawyer? Did you go to law school to help a client who has committed mass murder of other human beings with poisonous gases? Of course, someone should, and will, represent him. But why you, old friend?[17]

In an ensuing series of published exchanges between the two, Freedman makes the case for a lawyer's moral burden to justify his or her representation of pariah clients. The issue, Freedman argues, boils down to whether the lawyer, in his or her role as a lawyer, is morally accountable for his or her choice of clients or is merely a hired gun.[18] The "standard conception," Freedman acknowledges, is that a lawyer has no moral responsibility for the lawful means or ends achieved for a client.[19] And if the lawyer has no moral accountability for the lawful goals of his or her client, it follows that he or she has no obligation to justify his or her choice of the person as a client.

Freedman, however, rejects the "standard conception." Rather, he says, the lawyer's role is one for which society can hold the lawyer morally accountable. Because the lawyer is ethically constrained from trying to impose his or her morality on the client once the attorney-client relationship is established (for example, by threatening to withdraw if the client does not change his or her goals to conform to the morality of the lawyer), Freedman concludes that the lawyer's exercise of moral judgment must occur when the lawyer decides whether to accept the person as a client. And because that decision is one for which the lawyer is morally accountable, it is one that should be justified publicly.[20]

The moral accountability of lawyers to society, and the lawyer's consequent burden of public justification, Freedman contends, stems from the fact that "we are a profession that exists for the purpose of serving the public, and we hold a government-granted monopoly to do so."[21] Freedman suggests that the legal profession's historic failure to acknowledge this moral accountability and accordingly to explain and justify "the true nature and importance of the lawyer's role in American society" may even be a reason for lawyer-bashing in this country.[22] Thus, the lawyer's moral obligation to justify his or her representation of unpopular clients and causes may be viewed as part of our obligation as lawyers to "assist in maintaining the integrity and competence of the legal profession."[23]

In response to Freedman, Professor Tigar has made the case that no obligation—moral or otherwise—exists to justify one's choice of clients. For one thing, Tigar argues, to put lawyers under a burden of public justification is inconsistent with the notion that all persons, including the most notorious, have the *right* to legal representation.[24] If a lawyer must articulate a reason for representing a client other than the fact that the client desires a lawyer, the right to counsel is undermined. To be sure, the Sixth Amendment, which establishes a constitutional right to counsel in some circumstances, only applies to criminal defendants; one can thus say that this argument applies at best to a lawyer's representation of a notorious criminal defendant. But it is also a venerable, although admittedly not constitutionally enshrined, principle that anyone who can secure legal representation has a right to that lawful legal assistance. The argument can be extended, therefore, to noncriminal cases as well.

Second, Tigar says, imposing on lawyers a burden of public justification *invites* unwarranted attacks on zealous advocacy.[25] Of course, people are always free to criticize lawyers for representing certain clients; that is done all the time. To say that a lawyer has a moral *obligation* to justify the representation, however, is to establish, in effect, a rebuttable presumption that the representation is immoral, which only fuels the demagoguery.

Third, a lawyer's decision to accept a certain engagement will in most circumstances be based, at least in part, on the lawyer's assessment of the facts and legal principles relevant to the case. To the extent that a lawyer's obligation to justify the representation calls for the lawyer's assessment of the case, therefore, the obligation intrudes on the integrity and sanctity of the attorney-client relationship and the lawyer's work product. As Tigar put it: "I can no more be under a duty to make a public accounting of why I took this case than I can be under a duty to open up the files of all my cases to public view."[26]

At bottom, Tigar concludes, the lawyer's private reasonings are his or her own to share or not as he or she wishes.[27] As long as those individuals whom society has granted the privilege of practicing at the bar act within the legal and ethical bounds society has put in place to constrain that practice, society must trust those individuals with issues of morality to answer to their own private consciences.

Decision and Execution

Many of the greatest lawyers ultimately have decided to offer an explanation or justification for their representation of one or more unpopular clients or causes. In his autobiography, *The Story of My Life,* Clarence Darrow explains, among other things, his attraction to notorious criminal cases.[28] In *One Man's Freedom,* Edward Bennett Williams explains his representation of unpopular clients in terms of a greater need to protect the erosion of "the most basic principles of individual liberty guaranteed by our Constitution," for "whenever government infringes on any of these rights it begins with the weak and the friendless, or the scorned and the degraded, or the nonconformist and the unorthodox. It never begins with the strong, the rich, the popular, or the orthodox."[29]

Even Michael Tigar, though vociferously denying a moral obligation to justify his representation of pariah clients, has chosen to provide such justifications in moving terms. In explaining his representation of Terry Lynn Nichols, Tigar wrote an eloquent essay on the difference between the "system-called-justice" (which Tigar distinguishes from a true "justice system") and "justice properly-so-called."[30] Tigar describes his role in the Oklahoma City bombing case as trying to "see that the system-called-justice respects and renders justice properly-so-called."[31] Tigar's defense of his representation of John Demjanjuk is especially stirring:

> When the most powerful country on earth gangs up on an individual citizen, falsely accuses him of being the most heinous mass murderer of the Holocaust, and systematically withholds evidence that would prove him guiltless of that charge, there is something dramatically wrong. When that man is held in the most degrading conditions in a death cell based on those false accusations, the wrong is intensified. When the government that did wrong denies all accountability, the judicial branch should provide a remedy. I have spent a good many years of my professional life litigating such issues. I am proud to be doing so again.[32]

Perhaps the temptation is simply too great for lawyers—especially the types of lawyers who are inclined to represent unpopular clients or causes in the first place—to explain and defend the principles for which they stand. Perhaps lawyers fear their silence will lead to a negative perception that would be worse than the burden of public justification itself. In some cases, public justification of a righteous cause is completely consistent with, and furthers the goals of, the client and the representation. Justifying their representation of death-row inmates, for example, many lawyers try to expose what they perceive to be the injustices of the death penalty.

In the end, however, precisely because no clear rule mandates public justification, as a practical matter the Tigar position prevails. Each lawyer is left to decide on a case-by-case basis whether he or she publicly should defend his or her representation of an unpopular client or cause. Freedman's arguments about a lawyer's moral obligations to the public and the profession should be among the factors the lawyer weighs in each case. But the final decision must be a product of the lawyer's considered private judgment about, among other things, whether he or she believes a lawyer is accountable to the public for what he or she lawfully does as a lawyer, as well as what is best for the lawyer, and, of course, the client.

If the lawyer does decide to explain his or her reasons for representing an unpopular client or cause, however, care must be taken not to undermine or slander inadvertently the client or the cause. Even Freedman has made clear that the lawyer's moral obligation of justification (such as it exists) applies "within the bounds of zealous representation."[33] A lawyer representing a notorious client should never "apologize" to a disapproving public with the lame explanation that he or she never would have taken the case had he or she not been appointed by the court. If the lawyer cannot speak unapologetically about the constitutional right of counsel, the merits of the adversarial system in obtaining truth and justice, or the ethical obligation of lawyers to represent even unpopular clients or causes, then the lawyer should not offer any justification at all. For as in all questions of a lawyer's professional obligations and responsibility, as long as the client's desired means and ends are lawful, his or her interests come first.

Endnotes

1. Model Code of Professional Responsibility EC 2-27 (1980).
2. Catherine D. Bowen, John Adams and the American Revolution 356–57 (1950).
3. *Id.* at 362.
4. *Id.* at 384–85. Adams succeeded in obtaining acquittals for the soldiers as well.
5. Melissa F. Greene, The Temple Bombing 70 (1996).
6. *Id.* at 71–74.
7. Arthur Kinoy, Rights on Trial 97–127 (1983).
8. *Id.* at 123.
9. Lon L. Fuller & John D. Randall, *Professional Responsibility: Report of the Joint Conference,* 44 A.B.A. J. 1159, 1162 (1958).
10. Model Code of Professional Responsibility EC 2-27 (1980).
11. Morris L. Ernst & Alan U. Schwartz, *The Right to Counsel and the "Unpopular Cause,"* 20 U. Pitt. L. Rev. 727, 728 (1959).
12. David Goldberger, *Skokie: The First Amendment under Attack by its Friends,* 29 Mercer L. Rev. 761, 763, 767 (1978).

13. *See* Monroe Freedman, *Must You Be the Devil's Advocate?*, LEGAL TIMES, Aug. 23, 1993, at 19.

14. See Michael E Tigar, *Setting the Record Straight on the Defense of John Demjanjuk*, LEGAL TIMES, Sept. 6, 1993, at 22.

15. *See, e.g.*, MODEL CODE OF PROFESSIONAL RESPONSIBILITY Canon 4 (1980).

16. *Id.*, Canon 7.

17. Freedman, *supra* note 13.

18. Monroe Freedman, *The Lawyer's Moral Obligation of Justification*, 74 TEX. L. REV. 111, 116 (1995).

19. *Id.* (citing Murray L. Schwartz, *The Professionalism and Accountability of Lawyers*, 66 CAL. L. REV. 669, 672–74 (1978)).

20. Freedman, *supra* note 18, at 112, 116–17 (quoting SISELLA BOK, LYING: MORAL CHOICE IN PUBLIC AND PRIVATE LIFE 92 (1978)).

21. Monroe Freedman, *The Morality of Lawyering*, LEGAL TIMES, Sept. 20, 1993, at 22.

22. *Id.*

23. MODEL CODE OF PROFESSIONAL RESPONSIBILITY Canon 1 (1980).

24. Tigar, *supra* note 14.

25. *Id.*

26. *Id.*

27. Michael E. Tigar, *Defending*, 74 TEX. L. REV. 101, 109 (1995).

28. CLARENCE DARROW, THE STORY OF MY LIFE 74–76 (1932).

29. EDWARD B. WILLIAMS, ONE MAN'S FREEDOM 7 (1977).

30. *See* Tigar, *supra* note 27.

31. *Id.*

32. Tigar, *supra* note 14.

33. Freedman, *supra* note 18, at 112.

Judges and the Media 15

Hilton Fuller

THOUGH JUDGES, LAWYERS, and the justice system may frequently appear in the media spotlight, seldom do they shine. Generally, this is not because we are unworthy, though occasionally we are. Nor is it because we are not entertaining, for entertaining we can be. More often than not, we fail to sparkle because we do not understand how and why media function.

Most lawyers and judges are not skilled in public and media relations. Little in our education or experience prepares us for proper media interaction. As a result we often miss opportunities to present our clients, or the justice system, in the best light. Sometimes we are unnecessarily embarrassed.

In more than 32 years of trial experience, I have come to appreciate the importance of justice professionals developing strategies for "dealing with the media." What follows is a discussion of some of those practices, occasionally in the context of specific cases. Not all experiences with the media are pleasant and not all lessons are easily learned.

I hope that seeing events through a judge's eyes will benefit not only other judges, but also lawyers who constantly wonder why judges do the things we do. Judges, I hope, can learn from my experiences—some of which have been painful—without repeating my mistakes. Beyond both the scope of this chapter and my expertise are some items of genuine importance to lawyers, such as how to manipulate media coverage, either to protect or support a client. Needed help in those areas can be obtained from other chapters in this book, as well as from media specialists.

As for the judiciary and the media, one principle is etched in stone: Public judicial comment should be measured carefully. It is almost always unethical for a judge to speak publicly about a pending case. The consequences of inappropriate or misunderstood judicial comment are severe. With that principle always in mind, a trial judge should adhere to the fundamental guidelines that head the remaining sections of this chapter.

Be Honest

Never lie to, or consciously mislead, any reporter. If it is inappropriate to answer a question, just say so. Reporters are accustomed to hearing, "No comment," and the best ones respect it. Some judges refuse to discuss anything with any reporter, on or off the record. This is unfortunate, in my view, and reflects more a lack of skill than anything else. But being unavailable is far better than being dishonest; if forced to choose, choose the former.

Reporters are like the rest of us. Some are more trustworthy than others. Be honest with everyone, but save candor for those worthy of trust. Time will tell who they are.

Stay Out of the Headlights (You Are as Helpless as a Deer)

Bobby Dodd, the legendary Georgia Tech football coach and one of my personal heros, often was quoted as saying, "When you pass, three things can happen—and two of them are bad." When a judge takes the spotlight, many different things can happen. Most are bad. Judges should be no more comfortable in the spotlight than a deer frozen by the headlights of an oncoming truck. Something bad is probably going to happen, and soon.

Most reporters are pleasant people, and few take gratuitous potshots at judges. But journalists are not a court's public relations arm. They have no inherent responsibility to protect the integrity of the courts or the legal system. Remember that judges do not select the issues to be reported, construct the story line, choose the photographs, or edit the text or tape. Those who do so have professional interests that differ from ours.

There are judges who emerge unruffled from publicity's glare. But they are few and far between. Be careful.

Control the Manner in Which Your Comments Are Released (Assuming Some Comment Is Appropriate)

Some judges believe they speak better than they write. Some may, but most do not. Writing gives an added opportunity to think—and to have someone else review the thought process before it is too late. In those rare instances when judicial public comment is appropriate, consider the use of written communication, rather than unstructured oral comments. This means you should avoid, if possible, live or recorded unstructured interviews. No journalist will give you editorial control, and there is virtually no way to take back anything recorded by audio or video equipment. It stays around *forever.*

In *any* interview, do not say anything you would not want to read in the morning paper. Above all, do not ramble on the record. Unless there are clearly defined and understood limits, *anything* you say to a reporter can be reported and attributed to you. If a written statement from you is for some reason inappropriate, and it is otherwise proper to say anything, talk first off the record. Then you, often with the reporter's help, can review and determine what part of your thoughts will be on the record.

Of course, you must first agree upon the meaning of "on the record" and "off the record." All reporters who want to stay in the business will honor limits on quotation use. But just as with contract law, the key is making sure that both parties define terms the same way. Ask what the reporter means by "off the record, "background," and "not for attribution." Other chapters in this book more thoroughly address the various meanings of these terms, and how to discuss them with the media.

In any interview, beware of leading questions. A positive answer to a question such as, "Everybody in the courthouse thinks the county commissioners' reducing court appropriations was stupid; don't you agree?," could very well be rendered in headlines as, "Judge Doe Calls Commissioners Stupid!" If you must speak, make your own statements. Do not simply adopt those stated by the reporter. Exceptions exist, of course, to this and most other rules. In truly trusting relationships, it is often possible for the reporter and judge to assist each other in designing usable quotations. (This is a particularly valuable technique in harmless non-case-related subjects, such as the need for courthouse improvements.) In fact, if the judge and reporter trust each other, it is not inappropriate for the judge to suggest, "Why don't you construct a usable quotation that might survive your editor's attention; if I like it, I will 'say' it."

Make No Assumptions Concerning Journalism Ethics

There is no formal, generally accepted statement of ethics to which all good journalists subscribe. Hence, some confusion about the matter exists, as illustrated by a recent event.

An Example: Juror Contact

During a recess in a very tense multiweek trial, a seated juror reported that he had been approached in the courthouse hallway by a local radio reporter with the words, "I want to talk to you." The juror was startled by this contact and responded only by hurrying away. This event was reported to me. After talking with the juror, I asked for the reporter's explanation. The reporter saw nothing wrong, he said, as he was seeking merely an opportunity for a posttrial interview. My view was different; I believe the contact was clearly wrong, and perhaps illegal.

I wrote to the 15 or so broadcasters who had monitored the trial at one time or another and, without identifying the offending reporter or his station, reminded them that such action was improper. I was surprised to receive only one management response affirming that at that station such action would not be tolerated. I was reassured, however, by several beat reporters who let me know that they understood such contact to be wrong, both legally and ethically. Some wondered why the reporter was not in jail. Sometimes I wonder about that, too.

In the competitive scoop-your-neighbor-before-the-deadline world of modern journalism, there are meaningful differences of opinion about what are—and are not—ethical practices. Judges need to know that these differences exist. What seems clear to us may not be so clear to others.

Be a Teacher, but Be Cautious

Some judges complain that media treatment of courts is superficial, unfair, and frequently inaccurate. Often they are right. And often it is our fault. Sometimes it is appropriate—and perhaps even our responsibility—to respond to, or direct, media interest.

Because of time and space constraints, most legal reporters lack deep substantive understanding of their subjects. Often the media are satisfied with fairly superficial treatment, and so are their customers. Some reporters are legally trained, and others have useful training in other disciplines. But many others are not so well informed or blessed with the ability to view events from so many perspectives. The reporting of the most important event in your professional life may be done by one of those reporters. There are ethical ways to help reporters be both fair and accurate. Often you must teach—you must be an educator. A simple example follows.

An Example: The Krause Case

Connie Vance Krause disappeared. Ms. Krause's family and friends distributed flyers containing her picture. They called out publicly for help in locating her. The search to find Ms. Krause was reported by both print and broadcast media. A few days later, Ms. Krause's nude body was found in the trunk of her car in a public parking lot. This discovery, the circumstances of Ms. Krause's death, and the subsequent police investigation—which never resulted in an arrest—were matters of intense public interest.

Three months later, Ms. Krause's parents and siblings filed a civil suit contending that Ms. Krause's husband, Hans-Juergen Krause, should not be permitted to recover life insurance proceeds payable as a result of Ms. Krause's death. Mr. Krause, it was alleged, was responsible for his wife's death.

In the initial reporting of the *Krause* case, there was confusion about the different standards of proof applicable to civil actions and criminal cases. "Beyond a reasonable doubt" and "preponderance of the evidence" are basic legal terms, but clearly some of the reporters did not understand the difference between them. "If the district attorney did not find sufficient evidence to indict," they asked, "how can Mr. Krause be 'prosecuted' in a civil suit?" For trial lawyers and judges, the explanation is simple, but not so for the general public. I thought it proper to assist the reporter, so I made myself available for off-the-record discussions on this point. Perhaps the lawyers did also. In any event, stories with more depth and without attribution subsequently appeared.

Take advantage of opportunities to teach. Doing so may be quite helpful, and may also give you less about which to complain.

Understand That Judges Do Not Decide What Is "Newsworthy"

The *Krause* case involved money, power, sex, and crime. It also had fascinating legal issues. But it was the story of human tragedy and violent and senseless death that seemed to attract the media attention. Regardless of how important we think the legal issues are, seldom do they interest the general media. Except perhaps in esoteric journals, careers are not built—nor advertising sold—by reporting legal issues. The media is typically interested, if at all, because of a story.

This means that a reporter contacting you is following, or trying to develop, a story line. It is in your best interest to know what that line is. Ask, "Are you reporting on how efficiently and effectively I manage my court? No? Well, what are you after?" If the response is ambiguous, be on guard. On the other hand, if you seek media interest, you can supply the story line.

How stories get ink or air time is sometimes determined by design, and other times by accident. Often the determination is controlled by what else happened on a particular day. Many times meaningful items are ignored because the media did not know they existed. Sometimes the media need our help.

Consider Directing Media Attention

Occasionally I feel the need to direct media attention to issues otherwise missed. A recent example involved a case that reflected the ease with which assault weapons may be purchased in the metropolitan Atlanta area.

An Example: Drawing Attention to Use of Assault Weapons

Drug dealers wanted to "take out" a competitor. They visited a local gun shop. The potential purchasers were known to the gun dealers. Previously, they had purchased from the same shop at least two dozen guns (many more according to one of the men) and eight bulletproof vests. Apparently many of those items were shipped "up north" where they could be marketed for ten times the local purchase price. "You can't buy guns up north," the court was told later. These individuals wanted two more guns (M-11/9mm semiautomatic pistols, or Mac-11s) plus ammunition. After personal identification was furnished by one who had been brought along for that purpose, the transaction was completed.

Two days later, two of these young men, using these semiautomatic weapons, chased and gunned down two other young men—by mistake. The gunmen thought they were killing competing drug dealers. As far as is known, the victims' only mistake was borrowing the wrong car, causing them to be mistaken for the intended targets.

One victim was shot 25 times; the other, 17 times. The gunmen and the other gun purchasers ultimately were arrested and prosecuted. This case attracted little media interest; perhaps because murder is all too common. But I believe there are times when the public ought to know what is happening in our courts, even if the media are not excited. This was one of those times. I wanted to "say" something about assault weapons.

I was aware of the danger of improperly injecting the judiciary into the political gun-control debate. Under the circumstances of that case, I reduced that risk somewhat with a written statement filed as part of the court records. With the issuance of this statement, I gave the media a push into a story they were not otherwise reporting.

Beware: In a Media Feeding Frenzy, You Could Be the One Being Eaten

As judges and lawyers, we are intimately involved in the lives of others. Almost every decision makes someone unhappy. Sometimes the unhappy respond with public criticism. There is a temptation to respond. Avoid it.

Judges, prosecutors, defenders, and others have different perspectives—differences that are sometimes exploited by the media. But we are about the law, not personalities. Do not take sides with the media against someone else in the justice system. You might achieve momentary satisfaction, but our profession and the law will be demeaned.

Early in my judicial career, in response to severe critical and very personal public comment by our district attorney, I once released to the media a short written statement. This served to blunt public criticism of me, but it also had the unfortunate effect of shifting the story line to a public debate between the district attorney and the judge. In retrospect I now believe that the law would have been better served had I remained quiet, above the fray.

Ordinarily it is the judge's responsibility to take the heat, no matter the degree. The greater the heat, the greater the importance of quiet reflection rather than instinctive reaction. Take the heat when necessary even when it hurts. Without more fuel, the fires will quickly die. And the media will move on to another story.

A Small Step for Lawyers and Journalists, a Giant Step for the Law: Winning Back Public Respect

16

Lewis Wolfson

THE TEACHER WAS TALKING to the "television reporters" working on a story for the evening news:

> So what's the lead?
>
> Well, we haven't had a chance to read the material yet.
>
> You can do that in the taxi on the way to the interview. Did you get a camera crew? Remember: this is television. You need pictures. The deadline for the evening news is 6:00 P.M. and the clock is ticking.
>
> Can't we finish the story tomorrow?
>
> We're not talking about two weeks for a legal brief. This is an important story. The public needs to know about it. And you can bet the competition will have it.

The "reporters" were actually a group of Washington lawyers who had been thrown—sink or swim—into a television reporter's world by network veteran Deborah Potter. It was eye-opening, several of the lawyers later said. Previously, most had only a vague sense of the pressures on a journalist. They gained new respect for the demands in gathering and delivering news on a deadline.

The lawyers were participants in the *Dialogue with the Press* program, which brings lawyers and journalists together and gets out on the table the "exasperating, infuriating, and irritating" differences (as Rex Harrison put it in another context in *My Fair Lady*) between them. In this session, the lawyers had already gone after legal reporters Stuart Taylor of *National Journal* and a *Newsweek* contributor, and Aaron Epstein of Knight Ridder Newspapers with questions such as these: Why do you guys always get things wrong? You say that you have standards, but what are they? Don't you really just want to sell newspapers?

The fact-of-life this book illustrates is that it is no longer just an option but a necessity for lawyers and journalists to understand each other's worlds and learn to work together. The book offers much practical advice; but it is not about how to "handle" the media or publicize your case or get your own talk show. It concerns how lawyers and journalists can produce the kind of reporting that will benefit the entire community and help both regain the public's respect.

As we enter a new century, the public expects lawyers and journalists to inform and help guide them through a world filled with dizzying economic, social, and technological changes. For lawyers, it means meeting responsibilities that were scarcely perceived when most of them were in law school. Lawyers and journalists face a deluge of government, corporate, and personal litigation. Both are on the front lines of preserving treasured rights to free speech, fair trials, privacy, and social justice. The press and bar must now work together, for as Alexander Wohl notes in Chapter 1, they both have become "indispensable to the world and to each other."

Loss of the Public's Respect

Both professions also confront a humiliating loss of public respect. "Public sentiment is everything," as Abraham Lincoln said; "With it, nothing can fail; without it nothing can succeed."[1] Poll after poll shows the decline. Many Americans doubt that lawyers and journalists honor their own ethical codes. One could say that this ethical slide is a problem throughout society. But should that justification be good enough for two proud professions that ought to be taking the lead in changing that view? To their credit, both groups are debating their direction.

The mainstream press must wrestle with accusations of rampant sensationalism and even with defining who is a journalist, a problem most newspeople thought had been resolved long ago. Journalists wonder how anyone could think a partisan talk show host or an Internet gossip is indistinguishable from a *New York Times* reporter. But many Americans apparently do lump them together. "The media" are often seen as an ungovernable monolith. And the classic distinctions between reporting and commentary seem to have been lost in a sea of opinion.

The legal profession faces similar strains. The respect—and even awe—on which judges and lawyers could once depend have been replaced by snickers over lawyer jokes. They can no longer escape into the mysteries of the law. Law firms seek to explain themselves with glossy brochures, and even hire writers to translate legal language for the public.

But nothing has affected the profession's image more than television. Millions of people watch sensational cases like the O.J. Simpson murder trial on television. They believe they know how lawyers and judges operate. The impeachment of a president provided more lessons. We learned about prosecutors and grand juries and what may or may not constitute perjury and obstruction of justice. Millions of Americans "go to school" on the law every day by watching real and fictional lawyers on television.

Building Understanding and Trust

The chief question this book raises is: How do lawyers and journalists bridge the gulf between them and build productive relationships?

It has to start with trust. Lawyers do not earn that trust by trying to put their own spin on their cases or by thinking only in terms of their own or their clients' self-interest when talking to the media. The journalists contributing chapters to this book are saying: If you are fair-minded and clear in your explanations, if you show respect for reporters' operating rules just as they are expected to understand yours, if you get complaints out on the table, and if you seek a long-term relationship with journalists and not just a one-shot triumph, then you will build such trust.

The Hurdles

This book contains numerous examples of how mutual under-standing and trust can develop. Reporters especially appreciate lawyers' efforts to cut through issues and make balanced argu-ments without spinning, as the story about Buck Delventhal in Chapter 3 shows. And though lawyers often overlook the media's need to talk to a mass audience, they admire journalists' efforts to speak clearly and directly to the public. But major hurdles to understanding still exist, and include the following:

♦ Litigators usually feel a strong need to be prepared and in control of cases. They tend to see the media as an undis-ciplined, unpredictable wild card in the legal process.

♦ Sometimes it seems as though there are only two kinds of people in the world: those who believe they have been "burned" by the media, and those who expect to be. Lawyers need to refrain from such thinking, if real under-standing is to be achieved. Even with greater understand-ing, lawyers need to realize they are going to "win some and lose some" in the media.

♦ Both lawyers and journalists are short on curiosity about the other's world. Lawyers should try to put themselves inside a journalist's world, as they would with the world of a judge or jury member. And journalists, who generally love to get inside the life of an athlete or an entertainer or even a criminal, need to have the patience to explore the pressures inside a lawyer's world.

♦ Lawyers are far more likely to be interviewed by a general reporter than a legal specialist, and can be impatient about that. However, helping to educate a reporter usually is to the lawyer's advantage. And journalists generally do not bite the hand that feeds them.

♦ It would help lawyers to disregard that hoary cliché about journalists just wanting "to sell newspapers." Most take pride in independent news judgment and tend to see the business-side "bean counters" as the principal threat to reporting.

♦ Journalists have a lot of trouble confronting two of the public's greatest concerns: that the press criticizes everyone but itself, and that reporters are insensitive to the impact of what they report.

♦ Though many journalists are fond of saying, "We don't need to be loved, only needed," they are as vulnerable to flattery and as thin-skinned about criticism as anyone else.

Dealing with Television

Litigators put dealing with television near the top of their concerns these days. The O.J. Simpson trial was a watershed. Suddenly, many more judges and lawyers became worried about how to treat this "loose cannon" in the judicial process. Although television cameras in the courtroom are becoming commonplace, many judges worry that television will soon intrude in their world of bench conferences, sequestered juries, and gag orders to protect information.

Outside the courtroom, winning the publicity battle on television looms larger. Even litigators who deplore other lawyers' showboating can be mesmerized by television. Some begin to think they can try their cases in the court of public opinion. But it is wise to keep television in perspective. Public relations professionals often lament that dealing with journalists is not as much of a problem as trying to convince a client that there is no magic way to "PR" a story. Television's impressions can be fleeting. One or two well-researched and reported newspaper stories may drive much of the media's reporting of a case.

Winning with the Media and the Public

Ultimately, lawyers and journalists should not be adversaries, but allies in communicating to the public what Douglass Cater called that "essential truth" that keeps us functioning as an open society.[2] These are noble sentiments. But how can there be such a relationship as long as the "barriers and suspicions" (as Wohl puts it in Chapter 1) persist, and efforts to change the dynamic between the two rarely have succeeded?

Besides, many litigators wonder why they must have some larger view of media relations. Their job is to be advocates, winning for their clients and using the media to reinforce that advocacy. Such a shortsighted view can work against you. Too many lawyers tend to deal with the media as something an ill wind blew into the middle of their cases. They want to control the media—get a quick fix—instead of trying to understand it.

Understanding the Changes Affecting Lawyer-Media Relations

What Makes "News"

Journalists' views of what makes news changes. Not too long ago, covering the law amounted mostly to news from police reports and court cases. Except for the occasional sensational crime or trial, the subject was not high on the media's agenda. But television's increased dramatizing of the law, along with mounting public concern about crime, changed this. The media reported on local crime, the drug culture, violent behavior, and multimillion-dollar frauds. Television turned some litigators into larger-than-life figures.

Changes in Technology

Moreover, we are likely to see future changes that require adjustment and understanding. For example, if some are concerned about the impact that fixed cameras could have on the law, what would happen if reporters were to bring their own miniaturized video cameras to news events and interviews? Or, what if a study found that many Americans made little or no distinction between media reporting of an important case and Internet chatter about it?

Growth in Legal Reporting

Media reporting on the legal profession itself also has grown enormously. One reason is that lawyers have intensified their efforts to shape public policy. Mammoth lawsuits involving tobacco and asbestos are front-page news. The profession lobbies more aggressively for its interests. And law firms have jumped into the middle of partisan politics with campaign contributions. This means that on any given day, a lawyer might be called by a business, health, or political reporter, not just a legal specialist.

More Educated Journalists

Journalists are smarter, too, which surprises some lawyers. Some time ago, a senior partner in a prestigious Washington law firm called me with a stunning piece of news. He had just been interviewed by a reporter, he said, and she clearly was smarter than most of the handpicked law graduates that his firm had just hired. And, I noted, probably earning half the salary. More journalists are law school graduates, and others are quick studies on the issues involved in a story.

Use of Public Relations Specialists

And now that they must talk more to the public, some lawyers and law firms have turned to hiring public relations experts, as noted in earlier chapters. They want to look good on and in the news, and get advice about press problems. Some public relations people can guide you sensibly. But beware of the glib talker who promises a favorable spin on your case and television notoriety. Beware also of the overzealous flack who can make your firm look like a publicity hound. But the biggest mistake is to see public relations people as buffers between you and newspeople. Reporters generally do not want to deal with surrogates; they want to talk to you.

Where to Get Help, and How to Make Change Happen

The bottom line is that you need to be able to understand and work with journalists. Where can you learn how to do this? There is not a lot of organized help, as Wohl notes in his chapter. American University's *Dialogue with the Press* symposia—which emphasizes the atmosphere in the relationship—give lawyers a different slant on the world of journalists, and many participants say it helps them understand more clearly why the media act the way they do and how journalists might better understand lawyers.

Also useful are programs organized by the American Bar Association and community media/bar groups that focus on the First Amendment and court reporting. On the press side, the Society of Professional Journalists, Freedom Forum's First Amendment Center, and the Reporters Committee for Freedom of the Press encourage journalists and lawyers to talk and work together more.

But ultimately, the key to strengthening relations probably lies with today's law students and recent graduates. The television-and-Internet generation knows instinctively that the media could have a great impact on their careers. The *Dialogue with the Press* program offers practical help to integrate understanding of the media into law school curricula.

There is an even larger dimension to this critical relationship. Lawyers often are community leaders. They also are influential in shaping opinion about the media. Newspapers these days are eager to strengthen ties with the community and build a more loyal audience. And journalists debate the press's future direction.

You can influence that debate. How do you think the media can best serve the community? Should they provide mostly what the public "wants to know," or should they also tell us what we "need to know" to cope with tumultuous changes in the world?

The media's successes in recent years have added to our understanding of change. They include some of the most sophisticated reporting in press history by news organizations such as *The New York Times, Wall Street Journal, Los Angeles Times,* and others; C-SPAN's opened window onto government; and the popularity with large audiences of *USA Today* and CNN, both of which are trying to enhance their news coverage.

Conclusion

As citizens, we all have a stake in preserving a strong press. I once was part of a panel that was supposed to discuss business and the media with a group of young Silicon Valley executives. To our astonishment, they did not ask a single question about business reporting. Most wanted to understand how the media actually work, and were concerned about how the media affected them as citizens.

If you get to know journalists and get involved in the debate about the media, you may still win some and lose some. But in the long run, you, your profession, and the community will gain most by fuller reporting of the law and other issues. Judges, lawyers, and journalists can develop a new sense of accomplishment and regain the public respect they deserve.

Endnotes

1. Roger Norton, Abraham Lincoln Research Site, quoting THE COLLECTED WORKS OF ABRAHAM LINCOLN, Roy P. Basler ed., Vol. III, LINCOLN-DOUGLAS DEBATE AT OTTAWAY (Aug. 21, 1858) at 27. Available at http://members.aol.com/RVSNorton/Lincoln2.html.
2. DOUGLAS CATER, POWER IN WASHINGTON 235 (1964).

Index